GUIDE TO THE DESIGN OF REAL-TIME SYSTEMS

GUIDE TO THE DESIGN OF REAL-TIME SYSTEMS

MICHAEL F. ROTHSTEIN

Vice President, Data Processing Services
Responsive Data Processing Corporation
Mt. Kisco, New York

Wiley-Interscience

A DIVISION OF JOHN WILEY & SONS
NEW YORK · LONDON · SYDNEY · TORONTO

To my wife Nitza, for her enduring patience and continuing encouragement during the many uncounted hours, I dedicate this book.

Preface

My professional experience has been predominantly in commercial real-time systems design. From the beginning I found it difficult to obtain information that would help me to do a better job—that is, to learn from the experience of others when designing a commercial real-time system. The reasoning behind major design decisions were non-existent. Therefore, based on my lack of knowledge, I concluded that each system design was unique and that the type of information for which I was searching was part of a learning process that could be obtained only with experience. However, after having designed several commercial real-time systems I realized that what I was doing was similar to what I had done before. In each of the systems analyses I took the same recurring steps. My work progressed in the same sequence and involved basically the same type of analysis, judgments, and decisions. As far as I have been able to determine, these "steps" in the design of a commercial real-time system are fundamentally the same regardless of the manufacturer of the various system components.

This fact became more obvious to me while I was teaching a course on Real-Time Systems Design at New York University–Management Institute. To this course came students with varying levels of experience and types of background. As a result of teaching this course, I came to the following conclusions:

1. There is a great interest in commercial real-time systems. They are the systems of the future.
2. There is a need for a definitive work on the analysis required in the design of commercial real-time systems.
3. Little of the available information discusses the "why" of system design.

It was for these reasons that I wrote this book.

The purpose of the book is to describe what is required, and why, to design a commercial real-time system. Its goal is to develop an *awareness* of the effort, the knowledge, and the problems involved in the design of a commercial real-time system. This book is only a start, an introduction, a foundation on which the reader can build. It is intended for those who understand the basis of automated data processing, such as stored program concept, systems analysis, and the relationship between programming and systems analysis. It is a basic handbook for those who wish to obtain a more thorough understanding of commercial real-time systems and their design. It has been written for those who wish to learn.

As in many technical areas, there are certain aspects of real-time system design which require specialized treatment. It was for this reason that I invited my colleague, Bob Flood, to contribute the chapter on simulation. His extensive experience with simulation of on-line systems enabled a more authoritative discussion of this very important subject.

In the course of writing this book there have been several people who have helped, encouraged, and advised. Although the list is long, I wish especially to thank Michael B. Sichel for his encouragement, guidance, and ideas during the initial planning stages of the book. Thanks also to Selo Fisch, Elizabeth Thurlow, and Yaffa Yosiefya. It is with appreciation that I also wish to thank New York University–Management Institute and The Productivity Institute of the Government of Israel. It was in their classes, as teacher, that I developed and used much of the material resulting in this book.

Michael F. Rothstein

Mt. Kisco, New York
July 1969

Contents

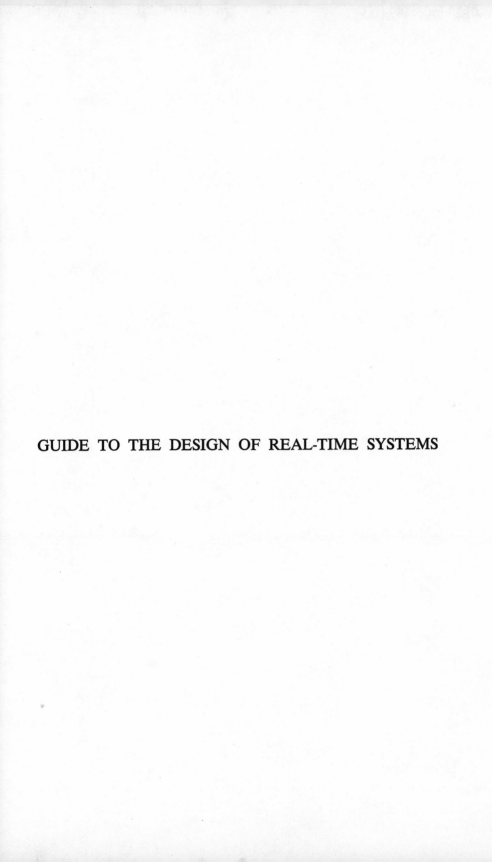

GUIDE TO THE DESIGN OF REAL-TIME SYSTEMS

CHAPTER 1

Introduction

"KNOWLEDGE IS POWER AND CONTROL, PROVIDED IT IS TIMELY, AMPLE AND RELEVANT. ONLY A BUSINESSMAN WHO KNOWS WHAT IS HAPPENING INSIDE HIS COMPANY REASONABLY SOON AFTER IT HAPPENS CAN ADJUST HIS MEANS TO HIS AIMS. . . ." [1]

Timely information is essential for the proper functioning of any business. One of the most efficient ways of fulfilling many of the information requirements of a business is by use of a real-time system. A real-time system is a computerized method of simultaneously receiving information from many geographically dispersed locations and processing and returning it within a meaningful period of time, seconds if need be.[2]

What does this capability mean to a business? How can it be used? A review of how management guides and perpetuates a business, viewed on a functional basis, provides the answer to these questions. From this viewpoint a business is a continuous cycle, involving four major functions: planning, implementing, reviewing and modification. The relationship of these activities is shown schematically in Figure 1.1. It starts at point A with the formulation of new plans and goals. These consist of planning for such things as new product lines and services, budget for the coming year, developing three and five year plans, expansion (or contraction) of expenditures for facilities and capital equipment and the like. Review and analysis of these plans by management results in major policy decisions, the next step in the cycle. Those plans and policies that are approved by upper management move on to the next step where they are interpreted and broken down into the many detailed plans and requirements necessary for their completion. It is

---

[1] Gilbert Burch and the Editors of Fortune, *The Computer Age and Its Potential for Management*, Harper & Row, 1965, p. 27, Courtesy of Fortune Magazine.

[2] This type of system is also called "fast-response," "on-line," "teleprocessing" as well as Real-Time.

at this point that first-line management and those concerned with the daily operations of the business become involved, for control of these detailed operations is their responsibility. Operating departments hire, buy, and produce in accordance with the specific instructions they have received. As each order is put into execution, reports and modifications based on problems and deviations from the planned schedule (represented by the smaller inner circle B) are channeled to first-line managers who, in turn, modify the schedule and do whatever is required to conform to and maintain an orderly "on-schedule" sequence of operations.

Trends, progress-to-date, and the overall status of daily operations make up the feedback information received by middle and upper management. It is used to review present performance and compare it with the previously made plans. Deviations cause management to take corrective action, which may include modification to previously approved intermediate and long-range objectives. Those modifications that are approved continue to implementation of management decisions, and the cycle is repeated.

The faster the cycle is completed the better the control that can be exercised by management. The more often that management is able to review the status of each plan and operation, the better (more quickly) nonprofitable and out-of-control situations can be detected and adjusted. Management makes its decisions based upon information it receives (feedback) concerning the efforts of the operating personnel and first-line management. This phase of the business cycle, daily operations and first-line management control, is shown as the shaded area in Figure 1.1. That is, daily operations personnel receive information from management (its requirements), act on it, and return to management information concerning the results it was able to achieve. Because of the expanding size and increasing costs and complexity of today's business, management needs to receive more information *more* rapidly than ever before. Unfortunately, the expansions that have created this need for more information, have the effect of delaying its return to management. Thus management is being forced to work in an increasingly demanding business environment with either less timely information or with timely data which costs more to prepare.

Computerized data processing systems have been an aid to management in attempting to solve this problem. Commercial data processing systems have evolved because they are more efficient. They do jobs faster, more accurately, at a lower cost than was previously possible. From the time of their initial acceptance, newer, cheaper, and faster devices and techniques have been developed—so that today there are many different

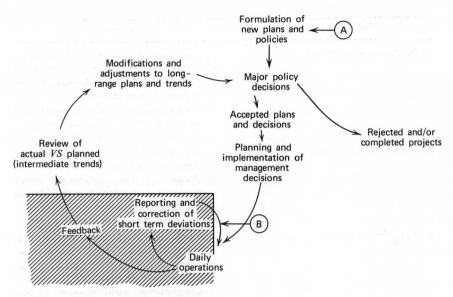

Figure 1.1. The business organization cycle.

types of systems—each depending on the data processing requirements of the user. The result is, of course, many different types of systems. These varied systems can be classified into five major categories. They are shown in Table 1.1. The column on the right shows the data processing environment for which the system is best suited.

BATCH COMPUTER SYSTEMS

Batch systems represent the more basic type of computerized data processing. Information is sent to the computer for processing, and returned in the form of reports or other types of printed documents. Before being processed by the computer the information must first be put into machine intelligible form. Batch processing's main advantage is that it manipulates information at electronic speeds while utilizing comparatively inexpensive data processing equipment.

PROCESS CONTROL SYSTEMS

Operations such as the monitoring of temperatures, the regulation of flows of liquids (oil, water, and chemicals), and electricity can be con-

TABLE 1.1

Computer System	Situation
1. Batch computer systems	a. Large amounts of data to be processed.
	b. Turn around time (from the time the input is createtd until the output is required) is not critical.
	c. Sending inputs to the computer and returning outputs from the computer creates no intolerable delays.
2. Process control systems	a. Inputs are continuous measurements of physical conditions.
	b. Outputs can result in physical action.
	c. Inputs and outputs can be distant from the computer.
	d. Turn around time is critical.
3. Time sharing systems	a. Many users, each requiring access to the computer for long periods of time.
	b. Immediate compilation and execution of programs desired.
	c. Comparatively small amounts of output.
	d. Inputs are geographically distant from the computer.
	e. Users can be from different companies.
4. Data transmission systems ("Batches" of inputs are transmitted for subsequent batched processing and/or the transmission of groups of processed output for subsequent printing.)	a. Large amounts of data
	b. Turn around time not critical
	c. The origin of the inputs and/or the destination of the outputs are geographically distant from the computer.
	d. Preferrable to maintain one set of data files.
5. Real-Time systems	a. Generally dedicated to one user.
	b. Turn around time is important.
	c. Inputs and outputs are distant from the computer.

trolled effectively by computers. Process control systems are designed to accept information from sensing devices. These sensors can be temperature gauges and other measuring devices which are continuously determining the status of one or more of the many factors that can affect the quality, or end result, of an operation. In a process control system this information is fed into a computer where it is compared with prespecified constants. These constants represent the acceptable limits within which the variable being monitored can fluctuate. Once any limit is exceeded corrective action is triggered by the computer. It can consist of an automatic readjustment of temperature, pumping, etc. (a closed loop system) or the transferral of information to those operators who will take the steps necessary to bring the process once again under control (an open loop system). Computers are ideal for monitoring these types of operations since they are able to take readings of the many variables affecting a process more often than is possible with strictly human monitoring.

TIME SHARING SYSTEMS

In order to reduce turn around time, time sharing systems utilize remote terminals for entering programs and tests. The environment of time sharing systems can consist of the following:

1. Many users, each of which are able to write and test their programs on-line. Time sharing systems have been primarily used by scientists and engineers who require immediate answers to a one-shot type of problem rather than running and rerunning of data-manipulating programs.
2. Users working in a "conversational mode." The time sharing system analyzes each line of the program being entered for correct syntax. After each line of coding, errors are typed out by the computer system.
3. Users entering programs on-line which are stacked for subsequent compiling and testing.

In order to service a large number of users, the amount of time made available to each is controlled by the central processor. This is called time slicing. The computer controls the input locations in such a way that it appears, to the user, that he has continuous access to the computer. In reality the computer is leaving and returning to each terminal. With this technique one computer is able to service a large number of input locations.

A time sharing system is similar to a real-time system in that it is a general purpose on-line system designed to fill *one type of data processing need for many users*. A real-time system is a specially designed on-line system used to fulfill a full range of data processing requirements, most often for a single organization.

DATA TRANSMISSION SYSTEMS

These represent an intermediate stage of data processing, combining remote data transmission with batch processing. Information can be collected at locations distant from the main computer complex. Based on a predetermined schedule a telephone-type connection is made and data is transferred into the main computer complex in one of two ways:

1. Onto tape and into the computer. Note that this method does not, at this stage, require a computer. The data tape is subsequently transferred to the computer for processing.
2. Into the computer and onto tape or disk for subsequent batch processing.

The transfer of processed data involves basically the same steps but in the opposite direction: from the computer complex to geographically dispersed locations. One additional difference is that the data could be transferred directly to tape for subsequent printing and/or punching or printed immediately and/or punched as it is being transferred.

Data transmission system can be subdivided into two major categories:

1. Off-line data transmission systems.
2. On-line data transmission systems.

Off-line data transmission systems

Under certain circumstances although there are remote data processing needs, there are neither enough transactions nor a continuing need for immediate response to warrant a "permanent" communication link with the computer. In these situations information is processed by

(a) batching inputs,
(b) establishing a communication connection (on a prescribed time schedule) for transferring the information,
(c) transferring the information onto a device in a computer room distant from the source of the input, and
(d) manually removing the transferred data to a computer for batch processing.

Once processed, the updated information can be returned to its source or routed to other locations.

The sequence of operations for an off-line system is shown schematically in Figure 1.2.

The advantages of this type of approach are twofold. Computer costs are decreased since only one central computer complex is required and one centralized set of files is maintained.

On-line data transmission systems

Once the connection between two points is made, transfer of data to (or from) the computer is possible with no manual intervention. It is

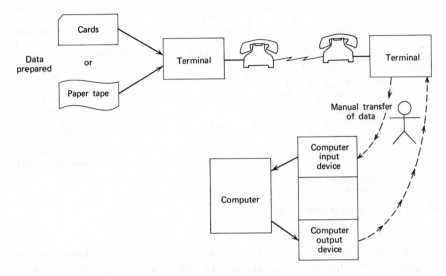

Figure 1.2. A basic data-transferring (off-line) system.

also possible to maintain a permanent communication link with the main computer complex, thus eliminating the need to manually establish a connection when information is to be transferred. This type of system is advantageous in situations where there is a slow processor, a large number of locations transferring information, and/or a large volume of data to be transferred. The transferred information is stored on an auxiliary device (tape or disk) for subsequent processing. This system does not overcome the costliness of the manual handling of data at the computer site, as the number of people required as well as the general confusion that can arise from trying to control manually the flow of such large volumes of information has not been reduced. The form for this type of system is shown schematically in Figure 1.3.

REAL-TIME SYSTEMS

Batch and data transmission systems operate in a comparatively unconstrained environment. Commercial real-time systems, however, must be able to process information in highly demanding situations (that is, fast turn around time, large number of inputs, and outputs to be processed within short intervals of time).

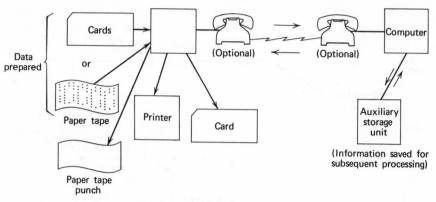

Figure 1.3. An on-line data-transferring system.

Most real-time systems maintain a continuous connection between the geographically dispersed terminals and the main computer complex. The input transaction triggers

(a) immediate processing of the input with the answer returned within seconds;

(b) updating of the central data files with only receipt of the message being returned by computer system; and

(c) a routing of the message to another terminal location, either on an immediate or whenever desired basis.

As with other types of systems, on-line systems can also vary in degree of sophistication. There is the on-line data processing system with "direct" file accessing capability. The more complete on-line data processing system includes an intricate internal data file crossreferencing capability, and is called a Management Information System.[3]

The on-line data processing system

Whenever immediate response (within an interval of time which could not be met by the previous types of systems) is needed, a system can be specified in which:

1. Information can be entered whenever desired.

[3] This type of processing of information should not be confused with Management Reporting by Exception. Reporting by exception is the automatic analysis of data for determining and reporting of *pre-specified* out of limits conditions.

2. The data is immediately automatically updated and stored on one central set of files.

3. The information required is transferred, again immediately and automatically, to the location entering the request and/or any other locations linked to the computer system.

This type of real-time system is shown schematically in Figure 1.4.

Management Information Systems

The state of the art has progressed both in types of equipment and functions that can be performed by a real-time system. Techniques have been developed and implemented for supplying all types of information to the user with no restrictions placed on his requirements, save that the answers exist in, or can be derived from, his data files. If the information is on the file, he can ask for such information as "for all customers who have ordered more than $10,000 in the last two months, tell me the number of times they have ordered item X2314, and the quantity of each order."

The procedure used for answering such types of inquiries includes the following:

1. An on-line real-time data processing system for accepting and returning of information.

2. A special file of indexes specifying the name and location of each *field* of data. These indexes and related data records can and should include most of the data requirements of the organization (a data bank or a data base).

3. A set of macros whose sequence of execution is automatically ordered based upon what has been requested.

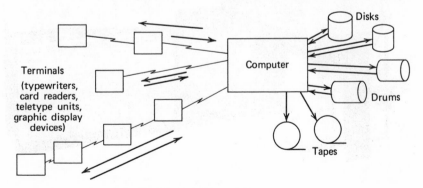

Figure 1.4. An on-line real-time data-processing system.

REAL-TIME DATA PROCESSING EQUIPMENT

The equipment available for performing real-time data processing are terminals, communication lines, computers and auxiliary storage devices.

TERMINALS

These are the devices which make available to the operating personnel the power of the computer system. The terminals are the input and output devices of the system. When such a device is physically located anywhere other than in a computer room, it is called a terminal. Inside the computer room it is called an Input/Output device. Their purpose is to

(a) facilitate the entry of data *into* the system, and
(b) receive information *from* the computer.

Some terminals are very similar to the card readers, card punches, and printers (see Figure 1.5) that one sees in the computer room of a batch type system.

Another type of terminal is the graphic display (see Figure 1.6). This unit is similar to a television set except that letters, numbers, or diagrams rather than pictures are displayed. Another terminal is the typewriter, similar to those used in any office. Although these, and others which are

Figure 1.5. An IBM 2780 data transmission (input-output) terminal.

Figure 1.6. The UNISCOPE 300 Visual Communications Terminal (Sperry Rand Corporation).

discussed in more detail in Chapter 6, are familiar to us, they incorporate the one additional feature that makes them more than just a typewriter, or a card reader—that is, the ability to communicate with a computer.

COMMUNICATION LINES

Communication lines are the bridge between the geographically dispersed terminals and the central computer complex. Their function is the transfer of information to and from these locations. Depending upon the type of line, these transfers are performed serially or in parallel (data simultaneously moving in two directions, both to and from the computers, on the same communication line). The rate of movement of information can range from a few characters up to thousands per second.

COMPUTERS

The computer's role in a real-time system is to

(a) receive (read) and send (write) data from external sources;
(b) check and process information; and
(c) automatically store, retrieve, or update data located on auxiliary storage units.

These functions are similar to those of a "batch" computer system. The operating environment of a real-time system, however, is more complex, with more types of devices to be serviced, each with stringent response time requirements.

Although there are special-purpose computers used in real-time situations, in most instances the real-time computer is the same physical unit as a batch processor. In fact, it is possible to have batch processing taking place concurrently with real-time processing, within the same physical device. In instances requiring high equipment reliability (when the interruption of processing, because of equipment malfunctions, cannot be tolerated) computers are duplexed. Processing can be automatically continued in the second computer when there is a malfunction in the first.

AUXILIARY STORAGE DEVICES

Real-time systems require large amounts of information. This information must be

(a) in machine-intelligible form and
(b) accessible when required (that is, with no human intervention between the moment the need for data is known by the computer and the time data are available in core storage for processing).

Tapes, disks, drums and tape strips (cram and data cell) are devices used by real-time systems, because it is neither economically nor technically possible to maintain in core storage all the data requirements of the system.

REAL-TIME SYSTEMS AND THEIR IMPACT ON THE BUSINESS ORGANIZATION

Of all the computer systems previously reviewed it is the real-time system that is capable of all of the following:

1. The controlled response (within seconds if need be) to data that has to be transferred long distances.
2. The storing of large amounts of information, accessing and processing it without human intervention.
3. The automatic correction, modification, processing and summarizing of information.

These capabilities can be applied to many of the problems and needs, and in a variety of ways, of all levels of an organization—by management as well as by the operating departments.

REAL-TIME AND MANAGEMENT

Management's decisions are based on an evaluation of the present situation in which the company finds itself. The way in which real-time systems aid management is in their ability to gather and maintain in an economical way, the most up-to-date information. In a non-real-time environment, information used by upper management consists mainly of verbal communications and periodically issued reports. The data for these reports are collected from many sources for summarization, copying, and distribution. For each report a cut-off point is established. Information received after this time is furnished on the next report. The time necessary to collect and distribute such information is calculated and used as a basis for determining this cut-off point. The date by which a report is required by management, minus the time required for the collection and compilation of the data, determines the cut-off date. In many instances this collecting and preparing of information requires considerable time, perhaps weeks or even months.

Prior to real-time systems, the time required for the compilation of a report could have been reduced by increasing the staff preparing the report or speeding its transmission by submitting the data by means of phone, special delivery mail, etc. All of these substantially increase costs. In addition, during the time required to prepare reports, management does not have a current picture of what is taking place. In fact, management must work with the old report until the new one, which will also be out-of-date (but less out-of-date), is issued.

An example of this situation is graphically represented in Figure 1.7. In this instance two weeks are required for the preparation of a report of inventory available for sale. Because of the time needed to copy information from the inventory records onto tally sheets, to collect and process it, a cut-off point, line A, has been set at two weeks prior to

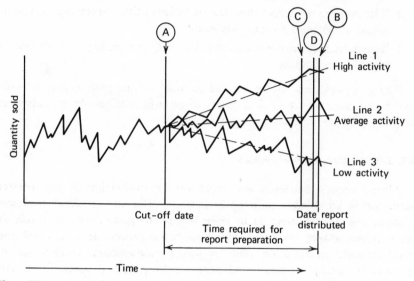

Figure 1.7

the distribution of the report. During the period delineated by line A and line B, inventory is being sold as well as replenished. There is, however, no reflection of this activity until the next issuance of the report. Sales during the two week period in question could have been greater (line 1), less (line 3), or about the same (line 2). Upon reviewing the report, management will make decisions as to materials to buy, manpower, production schedules, etc. These would be made sometime after point B but would be based upon data collected two weeks earlier (trends projected to point A could differ greatly from the actual situation two weeks later). A decision based on information only 72 hours old (line C) or only one hour old (line D) would naturally have a much higher level of confidence. A reduction in the delay between the time of data gathering, and its subsequent distribution permits reviews and adjustments much sooner than would otherwise be possible. The use of a real-time system makes it possible to achieve a substantial saving of the time required to prepare a report without a corresponding increase in costs.

With a real-time system, each location supplying data is connected to a computer by means of a data input device. Information required for reports is entered. Previous information is maintained, not by the operating personnel, but by the computer. By maintaining all required information, report preparation time is substantially reduced, and since the most current information is maintained by the computer system reports can be issued whenever required. Manual report preparation, per se, has disappeared. In addition to preparation of "standard" reports, automatic communication of exceptional conditions is also possible. As information enters the system it is compared with previously specified tolerances. Outside of limit conditions can be immediately referred to those managers who are empowered to take corrective action.

REAL-TIME SYSTEMS AND THE OPERATING DEPARTMENTS

In addition to supplying timely information to middle and upper management, real-time systems can substantially reduce the clerical efforts expended by operating personnel in the daily operations of a business. These improvements consist of the following:

1. Minimization of duplication.
2. Reduction of the number of errors occurring during the recording and transcribing of information.
3. Quick transfer of information.
4. Improved customer service.

Minimization of duplication

Incoming information necessary for the correct functioning of a company is received at one or more locations. Such information is usually in written form which, upon receipt, triggers various activities as well as transfer of data. For instance, sales orders trigger the activity of picking tickets and bills of lading. A new production schedule initiates the updating of inventory and purchasing records. Such information is often transferred through several departments, and whenever a record of the information is to be retained, what usually happens is that each of the individual departments involved updates its own records. Many of these individual files contain common information. In many companies, for instance, the Purchasing Department and the warehouse both keep records of the Finished Goods Inventory. The Sales Department keeps records of customers' purchases, and Accounting may also keep similar records of amounts paid and due. The justification of these duplications is usually explained on this basis:

1. If only one file is kept the information is available only to that department, since it is frequently isolated from the others.

2. Although the same data records are kept in departments that are near each other, each file is maintained in its own peculiar sequence.
3. Each file contains a certain amount of unique information.

In such an environment it is generally felt that combining these files would be too cumbersome a chore. The foregoing reasons are nullified by a real-time system of data processing. With centralized data storage units, information needs to be recorded only once. Data is available within seconds of request by anyone having access to a terminal. Time and money are saved because only one set of records is required, and they are updated at computer, rather than clerical speeds.

Substantial Reduction in Errors

Whenever information is manipulated there is the possibility of error. Papers can be misplaced. Information can be misdirected. Errors of transposition can occur; for example, 27 is recorded instead of 72. Telephone messages can be misinterpreted or an entry can be incorporated on the wrong line. As the material to be handled and recopied increases, there is a proportionate increase in the chance for error. Real-time systems reduce the amount of data manipulation and manual processing required to place information where it is needed and in the form desired. Many types of errors can be *immediately* corrected. A transaction can enter the system as soon as it takes place, and the computer will process the transaction as soon as it is received. This means that the message can immediately be checked for accuracy and reasonability. Reasonability checks are those which ensure that information is within an acceptable range. An order for 10 motors may be incorrect but it can also be considered reasonable. Whereas, a request for 10,000 motors would be an error if it exceeds the predetermined upper limit of a possible order. The system can automatically request correction to the information it has just received while the operator is still at the terminal and the data are fresh in his mind. A real-time system cannot eliminate all errors, but since it is capable of performing an immediate check on the transaction it naturally achieves a higher rate of correctness than it is economically feasible to accomplish with any other type of manual or computer system.

Quick Transfer of Information

A business organization is a composite of many interrelated units consisting of plants, divisions, branches, departments, sections, and so on. These units may be geographically dispersed, but regardless of the distances involved, each functions as a part of the total organization.

They use and transfer information as an aid to the completion of their duties. All information needed by the operating departments has a start and moves from one section to the next until it ends. Of the total elapsed time, from the time a document enters the first operating department until it is either filed or leaves (goes outside the organization) a major percentage is taken in the movement from the out basket of one data processing operation to the in basket of the person who is involved with the next step. A real-time system can reduce this total time by

(a) performing transfer operations, and
(b) shifting processing from individuals to the computer system.

Instead of a document moving from one location to another, the information is entered into the real-time system at the first processing station. The information then is electronically transferred to the next location in which

(a) there is a need to know the information that has been entered into the system and/or
(b) additional information is to be added.

Improved Customer Service

Today's business world being one of rapid change and competition, the company with the superior product is not necessarily the one with highest sales. Marketing knowledge and customer service play an important part in obtaining and retaining sales.

A real-time system is able to improve customer service. The ability to supply up-to-date information quickly and to process data rapidly, are benefits which can and do mean higher sales to a company. A customer may inquire "Can you ship 200 units of XYZ today? What is the status of my order? Will I receive it on schedule? Can you ship half of my order early and send it to San Francisco instead of to New Orleans"? By being able to obtain answers to specific questions the company that will prosper is the one that can develop and maintain good service by responding and acting quickly. A real-time system is capable of making information available from its files whenever and wherever it is desired.

In addition to its other advantages, a real-time system can be less expensive than the other means of processing data. Benefits such as better utilization of personnel, relieving the staff from tedious and repetitive work for more productive efforts, better utilization of assets such as less inventory or cash tied up in stock, decreased obsolescence and less capital equipment required, are just a few of the more tangible savings.

CONCLUSION

Since their inception computer systems have increased in size, complexity, and scope. With this increase in capability has come an expansion of the areas of a business being serviced by computers. Real-time systems, the most sophisticated of computerized data processing, combine and coordinate decentralized operations with centralized control. By efficiently gathering the information developed by geographically dispersed operating departments into one computer system, processing it, and then transferring the results to operations as well as to management, real-time systems play an essential role in fulfilling the information needs of a business organization.

CHAPTER 2

Commercial Real-Time System Design—An Overview

THIS CHAPTER DISCUSSES THE WAYS IN WHICH INTEREST IS GENERATED IN A REAL-TIME SYSTEM. THE PRESYSTEM STUDY EFFORT IS ANALYZED AND IS FOLLOWED BY AN OUTLINE OF THE STEPS INVOLVED IN THE DESIGN OF A REAL-TIME SYSTEM.

Integrating a real-time data processing system into a business organization requires change. Unfortunately change is something most people resist because it removes them from what is known and places them in an environment that is new, different, and unfamiliar. This condition must be recognized and overcome by persons within the organization with the authority to initiate and enforce changes. A real-time system can become an integrated part of the organization only when management (the people with the authority) is satisfied that it represents improvement and progress and can pass this satisfaction down the line. Management can become convinced only after their interest in a commercial real-time system has been aroused and they fully understand its capabilities. An initial interest and a desire for more information can come from various sources.

Outside the organization the source might be a computer manufacturer's salesman, professional meetings, social get-togethers, or trade and management journals. It is in professional and social gatherings that business people have the opportunity to exchange ideas. Management, exposed to these influences can become aware of the potentials and successful application of real-time systems.

Within the company, the suggestion might come from the systems group and/or data processing manager. This is a particularly reliable source, having the knowledge and ability to investigate and relate the potentials of real-time to specific areas of interest of the company.

Executives at various levels of management may perceive a need for

19

improvement and work "up the line" and thus generate a request for further investigation into "real-time."

Regardless of how this interest is germinated within an organization, it must be accompanied by a thorough understanding of the potentials and concepts of real-time data processing, and its relation to specific problems within the corporation. Such knowledge should be acquired before management decides to make a detailed analysis of precisely how and where these new concepts can be used. Furthermore, management must convince itself that the installation of a real-time system is the best way of increasing company efficiency and/or profit gain.

One way in which management can obtain this assurance is by undertaking a preliminary analysis, called a "feasibility study." This type of study is a small, usually a one or two man effort, and involves a review of present operations, problems, and costs. Conducting such a study not only requires an understanding of real-time systems (that is, what they can do and how they can be utilized) but also an ability to match this to the information requirements of an organization. On completion of a feasibility study a written report should be made to evaluate the advisability of beginning a detailed real-time system study.[1] This report would include the following:

1. Present data processing costs which include the costs of clerical help, salaries, overtime, as well as equipment and material needed to process and supply information to the organization.
2. Present problems which exist concerning the processing of present data, the number of errors, and the inability to obtain current information as well as the need for information not presently being requested.
3. A brief review of the potential of a real-time system as it relates to the solution of the present data processing problems through increased efficiencies and decreased costs.
4. The recommendations of those making the study as to whether a detailed real-time analysis should be initiated.

Should management decide to go ahead with the detailed study, the preliminary planning can be initiated. However, before it begins an extremely important decision should be made—the role upper management will assume in the control and review of the system study. *Direct management involvement is essential* for the success of the data process-

---

[1] Companies who are already convinced of the potential advantages of a real-time system providing benefits in efficiency and/or savings, often skip this initial feasibility study completely.

ing system. Independent studies that have been made concerning this question have shown a high correlation between the success of a system and the participation of upper management.[2]

One eminently successful method for this participation is the establishment, by upper management, of a committee consisting of upper management and the heads of each department of the company. The purpose of this steering, or advisory committee is to support, guide, and review the design effort. Besides ensuring the direct involvement of upper management there are other advantages to the committee approach. A committee composed of and representing all departments can . supply information relating to the problems confronting each particular department, and provide a more comprehensive picture of what the new system should do. In addition, when department heads are involved, the operating staffs of these departments will know that they are represented and that their interests will be taken into consideration.

PRESYSTEM STUDY DECISIONS

Establishing a chain of command is the first step that the steering committee undertakes before the detailed study of real-time system begins. The next is the appointment of a study-team manager. This person should have previous experience in real-time system design and implementation. A good background would include previous involvement in the design of at least two real-time systems and the implementation of one such system. An additional requirement would be some supervisory experience and/or experience or knowledge of the type of activity for which the real-time system is to be designed. The study-team manager will be directly responsible for the following:

1. The day-to-day progress of the system design effort.
2. Review and approval of all major system design decisions.
3. Development of a detailed schedule of design and implementation effort.
4. Preparation of periodic reports, to the steering committee and/or upper management, on the progress of the study, including all problem areas encountered.

[2] See "Getting the Most Out of your Computer" by McKinsey Management Consultants as well as "Computer Usage in the Manufacturing Industry," a year-long study of 33 firms by Booz, Allen and Hamilton, Inc. Business Automation, October 1966, pp. 53-57.

5. Staffing (whether from inside or outside the company) and training of the study team.
6. Infusing and maintaining cooperative relationships between the various operating departments as well as the data processing group.
7. Making recommendations to the steering committee on various technical matters.

Before starting these duties the study team manager, working in conjunction with the steering committee, must

(a) specify the scope of the study,
(b) determine the budget for the real-time study effort,
(c) develop the design schedule, and
(d) determine the advisability of computer-manufacture liaison.

SPECIFYING THE SCOPE OF THE STUDY

The purpose of this specification is to identify those applications and sections of the company to be analyzed, thus giving the system analysts an indication of management's fields of interest (that is, those areas in which management feels the study team can make major improvements to present data processing procedures). For each application a specific set of instructions to the system analysts must be developed. If the goals and limits of the study are not clearly defined, analysis may extend into areas that are not of primary interest to management. Limiting the extent of analysis at this stage reduces the time required to analyze existing procedures and indicates, with a minimum of effort, those areas requiring extended analysis. In addition it will aid in quickly revealing situations for which "real-time" solutions are not feasible. Those preparing these guides should therefore look upon the scope of the study as an *initial* set of instructions which can be revised. Redirection of the depth of analysis and areas of study can occur when the information being obtained by the study team brings to light previously undisclosed problems and inefficiencies.

The following is an example of a defined object (scope) of analysis which was used in an Inventory Control study.

January 20, 19___

SCOPE OF STUDY FOR INVENTORY CONTROL APPLICATION

Our company is interested in determining the applicability of a real-time system to control inventory, in lieu of or supplementary to its present system, which is presently in operation in the Production Control

Department and the Storerooms (Raw Material and Finished Goods) of Operating Departments 23, 47, 85, and 98.

During this phase, it is not considered advisable to review any of the procedures in the Sales Department as related to Inventory Control.

Management is conducting this study because it is concerned with the following:

1. Reducing the time required from the receipt of an order to the shipment of merchandise from the warehouse.

2. Maintaining an up-to-date list of all back orders which would be "readily available" to the production departments.

3. A method of processing that will reduce paperwork.

4. Executing all of the above at the lowest (lower than at present) cost to the company.

The inability of our company to make shipments to our customers as fast as our competitors has lost us orders. It is felt that information should be available so that rush orders can be filled and shipped within the same day.

Signed by

A. Jones [3]

cc: Vice President
     Study Team Manager
     Steering Committee
     Members

A. Jones
Inventory Control Department

DETERMINING THE BUDGET FOR THE REAL-TIME STUDY EFFORT

The budget for the real-time system study is closely related to the scheduling and staffing of the project. The less time permitted for the

[3] Mr. Jones, Manager of the Inventory Control Department, is a member of the steering committee. Since he is most knowledgeable of the problems of the department, he was given the responsibility of writing this first draft. Final approval should be granted by the entire steering committee.

design of the system, the more people and money required.[4] Determining the budgetary requirements of the study is part of an iterative process. The starting point is the first schedule developed from the initial estimate of money available and/or the date management wants the analysis completed. It is a possibility that the schedule developed does not meet the time limitation imposed, or that it exceeds the budget estimated by the steering committee. The study-team manager and the steering committee must then agree to modify the budget and/or the schedule. The time table must be revised until there is agreement between the budget and the feasibility of the schedule, that is, the schedule conforms to the budget as well as to the final time specified for completion of the design of the real-time system.

DEVELOPING THE DESIGN SCHEDULE

The study-team manager develops the design schedule which will be reviewed and approved by the steering committee. The schedule of the work required for the design of the real-time system, as stated previously, is a balance of the money available and the amount of work to be done.[5] There are many procedures that can be adopted for developing a schedule that would be

(a) easy to produce and inexpensive to maintain,
(b) clear and uncomplicated enough to readily indicate the status of the project even to those not familiar with the details of the design effort and
(c) one that can be quickly up-dated as changes occur.

PERT, Project Evaluation Review Technique, is widely used for controlling various types of projects, and has been used successfully for the scheduling and control of the design and implementation of a real-time

---

[4] When the amount of work to be completed remains unchanged and the time available to complete it is reduced beyond a certain point, the number of people required does not remain proportional (i.e., 4 people working 6 months probably could produce the same amount of results as 6 people working 4 months. But to complete the work in 2 months, would require more than 12 people). Reducing the time span beyond its most efficient point will require a disproportionate number of additional personnel—mainly because of additional communication and supervisory requirements.

[5] It is when the schedule and the budget for the study is being developed that the advisability of using outside consultants should also be examined. One can have the advantages of the consultant's specialized skills without having to hire a permanent employee.

system. It is a method of representing the various functions needed (called events) to complete the project. The organization of work to be done as well as the amount of detail used to describe each function is left to the discretion of the user. In fact, the more complicated and interdependent the events, the greater the applicability of this approach. One of the outputs of a PERT schedule is the specification of those items of work that are on the "critical path." Items on the critical path are those events the delay of which will cause a direct one-for-one delay on the time of completion of the *entire* project (that is, a one-day slippage in a critical event will cause a one-day delay in time of completion of the project). Using PERT to analyze the many items of work involved in the design and installation of a real-time system permits the study-team manager to concentrate on those items whose time of completion is most critical to the schedule. A PERT schedule can be developed and maintained manually, but computerization of a PERT schedule requires only a slight additional effort. To modify a PERT schedule produced by a computer, one needs only to change one or more punched cards, and the effect of even one delay on the *entire* project can be noted within minutes after cards are fed into the computer. Thus the initial schedule can be modified as more detailed information becomes available. A schedule that was developed utilizing a computerized "critical path" procedure, can produce reports giving the estimated earliest and latest finish as well as start dates and the amount of slack for each event. Slack is the amount of time an event (item of work to be completed) can be delayed without delaying the completion date of the entire project.

DETERMINING THE ADVISABILITY OF COMPUTER MANUFACTURER LIAISON

A decision must be made as to the advisability of obtaining computer manufacturer representation. During the early stage of systems design considerable use can be made of talents and personnel supplied by the computer manufacturer, such as experienced real-time systems analysts and programs that can be of help in the design of a real-time system. On the other hand, there are equally valid reasons for *not* establishing communications at this stage with any computer manufacturer, as there is an implied commitment that if the real-time system is found acceptable, it will be ordered from the manufacturer involved in the study effort. By use of consultants or "in house" talent, the company may take advantage of the full range of equipment and computers offered by a number of manufacturers, with no commitment being made to any of them.

This "going-it-alone" philosophy necessitates the development of a series of specifications by the company, which will be submitted to various computer manufacturers. This allows a competitive situation to develop which could result in lower equipment cost to the purchaser. There are, unfortunately, several disadvantages to this approach. One is that there will be little opportunity to take advantage of the afore-mentioned computer manufacturer's real-time know-how. Another is that additional work will be required on the part of the study team because, in order to comply with a tight schedule, initial transaction thruput, execution time estimates, and data storage (file) requirements would have to be taken care of earlier than would otherwise be the case. This information would probably be premature, since subsequent information that is developed could make such estimates absolute. Even if detailed information were *first* developed and then sent to various computer manufacturers, additional time would need to be spent re-viewing and evaluating the various cost quotations, and even with this additional effort, there is no guarantee that a better and/or lower costs will occur. In addition, should these lower costs involve equipment from several manufacturers, experience shows that problems can arise regard-ing the responsibility for equipment maintenance. Greater coordination and liaison efforts also will be required when an organization deals with several manufacturers during systems implementation and full operation.

Staffing the System Design Effort

The previous presystem design efforts required the coordinated efforts of both the study-team manager and the steering committee. The staffing of the study however, once the budget and schedule are approved, is the responsibility of the study-team manager. Ideally, the staff should consist of personnel who are knowledgeable in the present operating procedures of the company *and* who are also experienced in systems analysis. They should have an active interest in the work involved—that is, the study team should consist of people possessing the combined know-how of (a) a thorough knowledge of the capabilities and problems of the operating departments and (b) experience with real-time computerized data proc-essing. Should people with the attributes not be available, which will most likely be the case, it is preferable to recruit the study team from both the operating departments and the present data processing group.

Systems analysts should be recruited from outside the company if no people can be made available from the data processing department. If necessary, personnel from the operating departments may be temporarily reassigned for the duration of the system design effort as a lack of real-time experience can be compensated by on-the-job training and close supervision by the study-team manager.

DESIGNING A REAL-TIME SYSTEM

Determining how a real-time system will process information as well as what equipment will be needed for performing these functions requires the following:

1. Analysis of existing operations.
2. Specification of the new system.
3. Integration of the components of the new system.
4. Obtaining management's approval of the new system.

ANALYSIS OF EXISTING OPERATIONS

This phase of analysis involves the following four areas:

1. Studying present procedures.
2. Documenting the information obtained from the study of present procedures.
3. Formulating functional specifications.
4. Determining system performance requirements.

Studying present procedures

Processing information by a real-time system necessitates the modification of many processing activities. If these activities are presently being accomplished manually or by "batch type" computer processing, they must be changed in accordance with the specifications for the real-time system which can store data, update files, and calculate results with the capability of sending information automatically to where it is needed. The jobs of the typist, file clerk, dispatcher, bank teller, etc. will therefore, not be the same. The system analyst must determine what is to be changed and specify how it is to be modified. He has to decide which aspects of the application are to remain manually processed and which are to be completed by the real-time system. In an Inventory Control Application will the inventory record be updated by the computer system or by a clerk? Is the storeroom still to receive a hand carried request for goods or will the computer send a message so that the material can be delivered to the worker or ready for the worker when he comes to the storeroom? To find solutions to such problems the system analyst must obtain a thorough understanding of present operating procedures. One source of information is the existing procedural guides. However, the exclusive use of these manuals may give the system designer a distorted representation of present procedures. They may be out-of-date, lacking the detail required, or be devoid of references regarding unforeseen, extraordinary situations. If the analyst does not obtain a true, up-to-date presentation of the procedures involved, his specifications will, in turn, include systems procedures and program logic that will not fulfill the needs of the company. If the system designer does not have a first-hand knowledge of operating department procedures, the next best method is to collect information regarding the functions intended for the real-time system from personnel who use the data during the performance of their assigned duties. Since these people possess accurate knowledge of departmental activities, information concerning present transaction volume, file utilization, etc. is all accessible at the operating department level. A first line manager, foreman, or supervisor can also provide detailed information important to the study. In fact, specific departmental problems may exist that are known only within these departments. The information requirements of middle and upper management, of course, are different from those working at the operational level so the system analyst must also review the information used or required by the various levels of management. An understanding of the information requirements of the various levels of the company (operating and management) should give the analyst a complete picture of the flow of data throughout the organization. Consulting with all levels of the organization tends to activate interest and generate a positive approach and better acceptance of the entire company to the new system. It is also helpful in determining existing problems, that, in the opinion of those involved, reduce their job efficiency.

Documenting the information obtained from the study of present procedures

Each system analyst is sent to a section of the company for the purpose of obtaining information to be used during subsequent phases of the real-time design effort. Operational program logic, system performance, file organization, and terminal specifications will be developed from information supplied during the analysis of existing procedures.[6] If detailed information concerning existing procedures is not easily accessible to the system analysts, they will have to search for the data to satisfy their requirements—that is, they will have to consult the operating personnel. To minimize duplication of effort, information developed during the study of existing procedures should be documented so that it is readily available during the subsequent phases of design of the real-time system. The paper flow in a department, files used, physical layouts, and organization should be documented so that the methods used by operating personnel are easily understandable to people not familiar with the procedures of these departments. But what is the format for documentation? How should the information that has been gathered be set down? A standard preprinted form that is easy to analyze and fill out should be used so that the work of the analysts can be checked for missing details, if any. One type of preprinted documentation forms is S.O.P.[7] Basically, IBM's S.O.P. recommends a documentation that builds up information forming a hierarchy of detail. This approach permits people concerned with different levels of detail to deal selectivity with the level in which they are interested. For instance, the systems designer requires details that are of little concern to a member of the steering committee.

Once the documentation of existing procedures is completed, it is possible to finalize the real-time applications—that is, decide which applications are to be analyzed further. Some applications may be found to be impractical for a real-time system. What initially may have been thought to be a problem may actually not be one. It may be that an application has insufficient volume to be part of a real-time system. It is possible that a problem can be solved by means of providing better training for personnel or a change in existing procedures. A decision made at this point concerning the real-time applications permits subsequent phases of the design effort to proceed.

[6] There are basically two aproaches to the tasks at hand. One is to have each group of analysts study one application. The other is to have each group of analysts study all real-time applications in a given department. The latter technique demands greater effort from the system-design group. However, it minimizes disruptive effects on the operating department by reducing the number of people analyzing the procedures of each department.

[7] The Study Organization Plan is a technique recommended by IBM; See Chapter III.

Formulating functional specifications

Functional specifications are generalized written descriptions of the scope of each real-time application, which provide a guide for the operational program logic that will be developed in greater detail later. The specifications summarize the capabilities of the computer system, determine what part of the processing will take place outside of the real-time system, and establish the relationship between the outside environment and the real-time system. The specifications are also used for obtaining management approval and concurrence on the manner in which the application is to be processed by the system. They are also helpful in introducing new study-team members to the project, by providing an application-by-application picture of the functions to be performed by the real-time system.

Determining systems performance requirements

Analysis of existing procedures includes determining the volume of transactions. Operating personnel are presently processing a certain number of transactions each day. For instance they are typing x number of bills, selling x number of units, posting x number of bank books, checking x number of customers' credit, etc. A simple count of the number of transactions processed is not sufficient, and in addition, the transaction types that exist at present do not necessarily represent a complete list of transactions that will be processed by the real-time system. New input transactions will be created because new types of information that were not previously accessible, will become available to the operating personnel. Information must also be collected showing the growth rate in volume of transactions that the real-time system is to handle. Once transaction volumes have been determined they must then be projected in accordance with management's decision as to the number of years the new system must be able to function without modifications to the equipment installed. It is not sufficient to design a system that can process ten transactions per minute if these ten transactions represent the volume expected shortly after the system is operative and will subsequently be increasing. Transaction volumes must be analyzed, the peak period (the interval of time during which the largest number of transactions will be processed) for each transaction type determined, and then projected. It must then be ascertained whether any of the peak periods for each of the transaction types occur simultaneously. An analysis of available information plus a statistical sampling of the transactions can be used to determine the extent of overlapping of peak periods. The time interval in which the system being designed must be able to process a specified number of transactions in a given period of time is a decision that must be made by management (the steering committee). If a system design is developed that cannot sustain this level of performance, it is not a workable system. The most economical system that can meet this benchmark volume will be considered a satisfactory design.

SPECIFICATION OF THE NEW SYSTEM

The study effort, up to this point, have been directed toward determining the scope of the system, developing a schedule, and determining the problems and procedures of the operating departments. The emphasis from this point on will be on the systems design area and specification of the equipment to be used. Design will be accomplished stage by stage and then integrated into one totally functioning system. The following are the six major stages:

1. Specifying the central processing unit(s) (CPU) by
   (a) determining operating system requirements, and
   (b) developing operational program logic.
2. Developing the file organization.
3. Specifying terminal requirements.
4. Specifying line requirements.
5. Specifying the line control unit(s).
6. Determining fallback and recovery procedures.

The integration of the equipment that is specified will take place upon completion of the design of the main computer complex (CPU and files) and/or the entire system (CPU, files, line control unit, lines, and terminals). The processing ability of the total system will then be determined and compared with the system benchmark.

Specifying the central processing unit(s)

Determining operating system requirements

Maintaining the proper sequence of operations of the many interrelated components of a real-time system is the function of an operating system. An operating system is a complex of interlinked programs (routines), the nucleus of which resides in the main computer(s). In a real-time system the operating system must (a) have the ability to receive messages from a line control unit(s), at various arrival rates, with wide variations of message types; (b) provide storage for these messages as well as the data records for processing the same; (c) communicate with the various components of the system to permit processing of transactions and the transferal of processed messages to remote locations; (d) maintain an awareness of the status of the devices attached to the system as well as identify any malfunctioning units and (e) be able to transfer control of itself to the operational programs, and vice versa.

The operating system *polices* the computer complex. It is responsible for maintaining an orderly flow of messages, the accessing of the various components of the system by various operational programs, and notifying the "outside world" whenever there is a component malfunction. Operating systems vary in complexity and sophistication. A basic type recognizes the arrival and permits the processing of one transaction at a time. The more sophisticated operating systems incorporate a multiprogramming capability—that is, they permit more than one *partially* processed transaction to be present in computer storage. An operating system that supports multiprogramming is more efficient in that whenever a transaction being processed cannot proceed further (the processing must stop until a record is transferred from auxiliary storage), this waiting time is utilized for the processing of another transaction. This otherwise wasted time becomes processing time, thus the number of transactions that can be processed in a given period is increased. In such an environment the operating system thus helps reduce computer equipment costs without adversely affecting the response time of the system. In order to obtain these increased efficiencies, more main computer storage is required than would otherwise be necessary. Although this additional internal storage costs more money, in most instances this sum will be less than the hardware cost for maintaining the same thruput in a system having a less sophisticated operating system.

As operating systems vary from the simple to the very complex, the system designer must evaluate the various operating systems available and specify the one which can serve the real-time system best—that is, the one requiring the least possible amount of internal storage and/or the quickest possible response time. A systems analyst must, therefore, be able to ascertain the functions that are required by the operating system and match them against the functions of manufacturer-supplied operating systems. If no manufacturer's system meets these requirements, and if no compromises can be made, the operating system that is finally specified for the system could even be one that is coded by the user.

This is a costly and time consuming operation and should be avoided if at all possible.

Developing the operational program logic

The term "operational program (processing) logic" refers to the development of programmed instructions which will be executed by the computer for processing information. This logic must be developed in order to determine the processing time for each transaction type. These processing times will be used to determine whether the system is able to meet its thruput requirements, the criterion being, can the system process the number of transactions that will be occurring in the peak period? This operational program logic will in turn be used as a source document for the detailed flowcharting and coding of the programs. At this stage, however, the amount of detail that is required, is only that which will clearly show the steps, in the processing of the transaction, at which the following will take place:

(a) input transaction received
(b) output transaction written
(c) the execution of input-output control and other operating system routines
(d) auxiliary storage transfers to and from computer memory
(e) logic splits (decisions that will be made)

The various blocks of uninterrupted processing must contain enough detail so that an experienced person, knowledgeable in the workings of the computer being reviewed, can estimate the number of instructions per block. This number of instructions multiplied by the average execution time per instruction will yield the timings for each execution of an operational program block. Input-Output, operating system execution, and I-O record transfer times must be added to develop the total processing time for each transaction. Unless the computer is one of a product line which utilizes the same instruction set in different model sizes and speeds, it is very desirable that the programming logic be developed in a nonmachine oriented format. This precaution is advisable as it may later develop that the computer chosen is not fast enough, does not have enough internal storage, or possibly is too large. If such is the case, another machine with new timings can be substituted without having to redo the operational program logic flow.

If the study team is large enough, there will be more than one function of the real-time system design taking place at once. For example, it is possible that the operational program logic development and the data record formatting (file organization and sizing) will occur at the same time. In such circumstances, there must be interaction between the groups. When developing the operational program processing logic, the functional specifications as well as the information flow derived during the study of the present procedures will be used as guides. A combination of the two will constitute the initial draft of the real-time system processing logic.

Developing the file organization

In order for the system to process and answer input transactions on an immediate on-demand basis, data will have to be automatically accessible to the computer. This information must be contained in "on-line storage." Which information must be made available on demand, and how it is to be stored, is determined as follows:

1. Using the information obtained from the study of present procedures, decide which files, and file records, are to be accessed by the computer.
2. Determine which files are to be accessible during the real-time day.
3. Ascertain which data records are to be placed on random access type devices and which on sequential devices.
4. Determine total random access storage requirements for all data records (taking future expansion into consideration).
5. Determine storage requirements for miscellaneous functions such as
   (a) programs,
   (b) scratch records,
   (c) indexes,
   (d) unusable storage,
   (e) fallback and recovery,
   (f) areas required for overflow and/or addition of records, and
   (g) duplicate records.
6. Using these storage requirements, determine the kind and number of units that are needed to store this volume of information.
7. Learn the physical characteristics of the various devices.
8. Combine these characteristics with an addressing technique and determine the access and transfer times for each record request.

On completion of documentation, the file design area will be considered to be complete. Future investigation, however, may show that either additional or appreciably less storage is required or that the device(s) is (are) too slow. If so, a recycling of the file design effort will be required.

Specifying terminal requirements

The terminal is the communicating device which enables the user to send and receive messages to and from the computer system. Terminals can be as distant as desired from the main computer. Input-Output devices of many differing types (card readers, typewriters, visual display units, paper tape units, etc.) can all be connected to the computer. The system analyst assigned to the task of specifying terminal requirements must choose the appropriate types of terminal devices and the location of each. To accomplish these objectives the system designer should first analyze the documentation of existing procedures. The following information contained therein is relevant for determining the terminal requirements of the system:

(a) the information presently entering and leaving the existing system,

(b) the locations from which messages are received and the places to which they are sent,

(c) the information that is added (new fields created) during various stages of the flow and when these additions take place,

(d) the number of transactions that are sent and received at each step in the flow.

A study of the above information will enable the analyst to decide the type of devices (e.g., card reader or typewriter) needed. He will also be able to recommend the locations of these units by analyzing the tasks that will be performed by operating personnel when they are aided by a real-time system.

The message volumes that were developed previously during the study of existing procedures are analyzed next, to determine if there is enough volume for more than one terminal. If the volume is high, it is possible that multiple terminals will be required at a specific location. The results of this analysis plus the information regarding the location and type of terminals, will be used to determine the line requirements.

Specifying line requirements

Terminals are able to send or request information of the system only after they have been connected to the main computer complex by means of communication lines. Depending upon the needs of the operating personnel, this access to the computer system can be permanent (leased lines) or on an "as required" basis (dial-up arrangement). The specification of the terminals is necessary for determining the type (full duplex, half-duplex) and the speed of the lines. Since each terminal has a specified rated speed, the lines required to transfer data from the device to the computer complex can be readily determined. When determining the line requirements, the system analyst must develop a network of lines which will transfer information to and from the operating personnel within a reasonable period of time and at a minimum cost.

There are many mathematical techniques as well as network design programs that are available to determine the line configuration which will handle the estimated transaction volumes. Various types of lines may be required since the various devices that have been selected may require different line speeds. It should be determined if other devices can be substituted so that the number of different lines can be reduced, thus effectively reducing the total costs. The cost of the network is based upon the tariffs,[8] distances, and types of lines. This information can be obtained from any of the companies, called common carriers, who supply communication services.

Specifying the line control unit(s)

Synchronization of transmission speeds and code conversion are two reasons why a special purpose device is needed to connect the transmission lines to the main computer complex. There are many kinds of units available, each with different characteristics. Knowledge of the lines required for the real-time system is a prerequisite to the specification of the number and types of line control units that are needed. Each unit has a limitation as to the number of lines permissible, as well as the maximum speed of any line. A study must be made of the functions that available units can perform. Code conversion, message logging, message formatting, and editing are functions that can be performed by some types of line control units. A list of required functions should be developed, and the line control unit(s) that is (are) specified should perform those functions needed by the system at the lowest cost.

Determining fallback and recovery procedures

One of the tasks in the design of a real-time system is to specify the action to be taken in the event of a malfunction of one or more of the

---

[8] Tariffs are costs, charged by common carriers for communication service which have been previously filed and approved by the Federal Communications Commission.

components. Good system design provides solutions to the problems of

(a) recognizing malfunctioning unit(s) in the system,
(b) specifying the remedial action to be taken, and
(c) reintegrating functioning unit(s) into the system.

Malfunctions may occur in terminals, lines, line control units, computer(s), and files. They may occur to any one of them individually or in any combination. The systems designer must anticipate the types of malfunctions that can take place and provide alternate procedures. The system must possess the ability to adapt quickly to various conditions and continue processing. In some instances, the entire system must be taken off-line (disconnected from the system) because of improper performance of a key unit. Once a unit is again operating properly, the system designer must specify procedures to reintegrate the unit in its correct place within the system, ensuring the completed processing of *all* transactions and records. For example, records may not have been updated, because the files were not accessible to the system. Recovery procedures must complete the updating of all records prior to the reintegration of the repaired units(s) into the total system.

Development of fallback and recovery procedures, will assure management that the company can continue to function when a part of its information processing system becomes inoperative.

A supplementary technique for ensuring increased continuous information availability is by means of duplexing some (or all) of the system. Duplexing is the use of a redundant unit for the same purpose as the original one. If one malfunctions, the other is available. Although this approach increases equipment costs, it aids in transaction processing in that

(a) increased thruput is possible when both units are functioning properly, since they can both be used for processing,
(b) functions can be divided between the units. (For example, each may process only specified transaction types.)

INTEGRATING THE COMPONENTS OF THE NEW SYSTEM

Many of the previously reviewed functions are performed in parallel (with each other). Each system analyst determines that his area performs as required. Once each has completed his work, it is necessary to determine whether the equipment selected is capable of meeting the performance level specified by management—that is, can it process the number of transactions required in the time allocated? Can it meet the benchmark that was set during the development of system performance requirements.

This final evaluation consists of tracing each message path through the system from its entrance to its complete processing—component by component, logical section by logical section. The total time for each transaction type can be added for the transactions occurring during the peak period. It is possible, by using this "gross" technique, to arrive at the conclusion that the system can meet its performance requirements. There will be instances, however, in which this simple approach will indicate that the system has not met performance requirements, thus necessitating the possible redesign of the system. If the operating system selected permits multiprogramming, a more detailed timing may show that the system does meet system requirements. In a multiprogramming environment (e.g., processing two or more transactions concurrently) the total elapsed time during which several messages are entering and leaving the system is *not* the sum of the transit times of the individual messages. Ascertaining this overlapping of functions may require the use of either advanced analytical techniques or the development of a simulation model in order to determine the processing level (thruput) of the system. If the results of such an analysis show that the system cannot process all transactions entering the system during the peak period, the redesign of one or more sections of the system must take place. Eventually, all required changes to the initially designed system will be completed. The resultant system will be one which, to the best available knowledge, will perform in accordance with management's specifications. Since the system design is being based upon a forecast of future requirements, the systems designer should determine, as time progresses, and implementation begins, whether the projections are accurate. Comparisons should be made to ascertain the extent to which actual operations deviate from the forecast. Such deviations may require the addition or modification of units in the system, such as the addition of disk files or data channels, rearrangement of existing units, etc. Provisions for such changes should be planned to the completion of the systems design effort.

OBTAINING MANAGEMENT'S APPROVAL OF THE NEW SYSTEM

Implementation of the new system can begin once official approval is obtained from management. Before this endorsement can be secured the study team must

(a) establish the cost of system,
(b) document the study teams findings, and
(c) present the new system to management.

Establishing the cost of the system

Management will not approve any new system until it knows how much it will cost. These costs consist of the following:

1. Hardware-equipment costs (terminals, lines, files, and computers).
2. Software-programming costs. Salaries, and expenses for the coding and testing of programs. Also included are the salaries of maintenance programmers and systems operators once the system is installed.
3. Training costs. The cost of training the operating personnel so that they will be able to operate the terminals correctly.
4. Conversion costs. The costs of converting the present system (files, forms, procedures, etc.) into a structure that will be compatible with the new system.
5. Miscellaneous costs. These include such items as paper, electricity, site preparation, air conditioning and the like.

Included with the above should be the displaceable costs; the savings (tangible as well as intangible) which will counterbalance part, if not all, of the cost of the new system. These represent the estimated dollar savings of the newly designed real-time system *once it is running*. Management must be appraised of the fact that during the final stages of implementation there will be two systems running concurrently. One, the presently operating system and the other, the newly installed real-time system in the final stages of checkout.

Documenting the study team's findings

The documentation of the findings of the systems design group is the final study report. Included should be

(a) a description of how the system will process each transaction type,
(b) the flow of this processing,
(c) the hardware components needed,
(d) description of equipment utilization,
(e) cost of the system,
(f) recovery and fallback procedures,

    (g) all assumptions and forecasts,
    (h) manner of arriving at conclusions,
    (i) premises used to develop the systems benchmark, and
    (j) present procedures.

In addition, an implementation schedule should be included. It should contain

    (a) the delivery dates of system components,
    (b) personnel training required and schedule of coding and testing of the individual programs,
    (c) the order in which applications will be placed on the system and made fully operational, and
    (d) background requirements and experience of operating personnel and computer console operators as well as the training required for implementation. (Included should be the specification of procedures to be used by these personnel.)

While the study team is preparing the final study report, the computer manufacturer that will be supplying the equipment for the new system should be preparing a written proposal of equipment to be supplied. The price of the equipment is included as well as the obligations of both parties—the manufacturer and the user.

Presenting the new system to management

Obtaining approval of the new system usually involves a verbal presentation to upper management and the steering committee. How the system will work, its cost, and the implementation schedule are reviewed. It is management's approval that will initiate the start of the implementation of the system.

CONCLUSION

The items in the development of a real-time systems study, as reviewed in this chapter, can be summarized as follows:

1. Initial investigation (feasibility study) of data flow, costs and efficiencies of present existing procedures
2. A favorable response of management recommending further investigation into a real-time system study.
3. The establishment of a steering committee.
4. Appointment of a study-team manager.
5. Specification of the scope of the study.

6. Development of a budget and study schedule.
7. Staffing and training of the study team.
8. Decision as to computer manufacturer liaison.

Upon the successful conclusion of the predesign phase of the system study, the actual design of the new system can be initiated. The steps (functions to be performed) can be divided into the four major categories shown in the following Table 2.1.

TABLE 2-1 Design of a Real-Time System

Major Categories	Parallel Operations
1. Analysis of existing system	a. Studying present procedures
	b. Documenting existing procedures
	c. Formulating functional specifications
	d. Determining system performance requirements
2. Specification of the new system	a. Specifying the central processing unit(s)
	1. Determining operating system
	2. Developing operational program logic
	b. Developing the file organization
	c. Specifying terminal requirements
	d. Specifying line requirements
	e. Specifying the line control unit
	f. Determining fallback and recovery procedures
3. Integrating the system	a. Determining total system processing throughput and component utilization
4. Preparations for management approval	a. Finalizing the cost of the system
	b. Documenting the study team's findings
	c. Presenting the new system to management

The following chapters will examine, in detail, each of these areas (of real-time system design), concluding with an examination of the implementation of a real-time system.

CHAPTER 3

Studying Present Procedures

COMMERCIAL REAL-TIME SYSTEMS COMBINE A COMPANY'S INFORMATION REQUIREMENTS WITH THE LATEST DATA PROCESSING TECHNOLOGY. DETERMINING THOSE FUNCTIONS THAT THE REAL-TIME SYSTEM CAN PERFORM MOST EFFICIENTLY REQUIRES AN UNDERSTANDING OF EXISTING PROCEDURES AND REQUIREMENTS. THIS CHAPTER ANALYZES THIS PHASE OF A COMMERCIAL REAL-TIME SYSTEM DESIGN.[1]

INTRODUCTION

Non-real-time systems, whether manual or batch type working in unison with manual procedures, possess serial characteristics. Certain action triggers the start of the flow, such as the operator receiving data from outside the company. After the completion of one step, information is filed and/or forwarded to the next process in the flow. This flow can be represented as a continuous stream of information where an action follows its preceding one, in a prescribed order (see Figure 3.1).

Even if the information is routed directly to the next step in sequence, delays occur either during or between the intervals of the actions in the flow. Delays may be caused by external events (waiting for internal or external mail deliveries) or by human limitations (interruptions as well as inability of a worker to handle more than one item at a time regardless of how many items are pending). These delays represent a major portion of the total time required to process and transfer data from the point of entry into the system until its final disposition.

When designing a batch type computer system, one need not modify

---

[1] The techniques for developing this information are closely allied to those used in designing a batch type system. Those readers with batch type system design experience may find they are familiar with much of the information developed in this chapter. They may, therefore, wish to review first the summary at the end of the chapter to determine the extent to which they may derive additional information from this chapter.

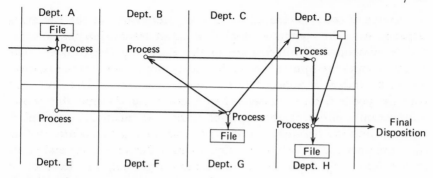

Figure 3.1. Present system flow.

the flow of information but simply reroute it to include the computer within the sequence of operations. In order to utilize the processing capabilities inherent in a commercial real-time system, it is highly probable that present procedures will be modified. This means eliminating duplication, automating existing files, and rerouting the flow of data. Many possibilities exist; for instance, as far as improving the flow of information is concerned, the systems analyst may decide, based upon his findings, to interface with the computer system in a manner shown in Figure 3.2a.

This type of flow has proved itself for situations in which documents are to be accompanied with the goods. For example, the transaction denoting

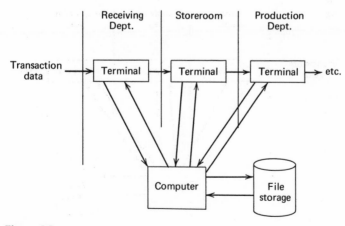

Figure 3.2a

the receipt of goods is entered in the computer system at the Receiving Department. The computer checks the input transaction for accuracy and returns updated information to the Receiving Department. The output from the computer is noted by the employee on the input (source) document and/or is attached to the source document. The document with the goods is then transferred to a storeroom. During this period information concerning the types of items and quantities received is inputted into the real-time system. The computer then updates its files (the inventory file as well as the Open Order Purchase File) and sends to the Receiving Department information regarding the location to which the goods are to be moved. When the goods are transferred into the storeroom, information is then entered into the system by the store-keeper. Systems output would be data, such as destination and arrival time which concern the Production Departments that are to receive these goods.

Figure 3.2*b* shows a different type of information flow. With this flow, interdepartmental information is transmitted only by the real-time system. The employee needs only to enter the basic input data and the computer system automatically updates its records and sends information to the next step(s) in the "real-time" flow. Sales order entry systems, reservation and bank deposit system operate in this manner. In Figure 3.2*b* the transaction is entered by the Sales Department, and errors and/or requests for missing data are returned to the Sales Department. Once accepted by the computer, the input transaction triggers the updating

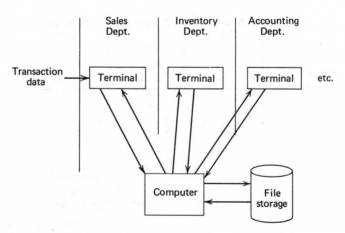

Figure 3.2b

of related files and the sending of messages to the Finished Goods Inventory and Accounting Departments. These messages initiate the movement of goods to fill the customer's orders and the preparation of the invoice.

Despite these alternatives, the flow of data should only be changed whenever better results can be obtained. Improvements can be integrated into a new system only if the study-team analysts

(a) know how information is presently being manipulated (processed),

(b) understand the purpose of the present system (why the data is processed), and

(c) can learn the problems facing personnel at all levels in the organization structure.

The study of present procedures is the essential prerequisite to specifying the functions to be performed by a real-time system. This study involves

(a) initial preparations,

(b) analysis of present operations, and

(c) documentation for subsequent analysis.

INITIAL PREPARATIONS

Because of his previous training and experience the study-team manager should be the person responsible for the preparations necessary for the beginning of the actual study of present procedures. He must

(a) contact the operating departments,

(b) specify documentation requirements,

(c) train the study-team members, and

(d) make work assignments.

Contacting the operating departments

During the prestudy development phase the study-team manager has been working with management and the steering committee. He has been involved with the company's decisions concerning the applications to be studied and their scope, as well as the reasons for including them in the system study. He has also met the company's departmental managers and discussed with them and the steering committee the work required to design a real-time system.

The study-team manager must, for each application that has been selected for analysis, complete a list of

(a) the departments that are to be visited, and

(b) the names of those people, in each department, who will be responsible for information being made available to the assigned analysts. (After the initial contact with the system analyst it is they who will be arranging appointments for subsequent departmental interviews, meetings, etc.).

The study-team manager maintains contact with each departmental representative and notifies him when analyst(s) are assigned as well as the time of their visit to his department.

Specifying documentation requirements

Documentation requirements must be specified in detail by the study-team manager because of the importance and amount of information that is required. The documentation will be used by those who will be

(a) determining the functional specifications of the new system,

(b) responsible for the program logic specifications, and

(c) responsible for the review and approval of the real-time system.

Documentation requirements, because of their importance, should be specified in writing. These specifications should enumerate

(a) what information is needed; why it is necessary—that is, the uses to which it will be put, and

(b) the level of detail required.

Information requirements, what and why needed

Many different types of information are required when designing a commercial real-time system. Figure 3.3 lists, in tabular form, the major categories of information that must be obtained. Alongside each is given the reason(s) why information is needed.

The level of detail required

In addition to determining the form in which the present system is to be documented, the study-team manager must also specify the level of detail required. The emphasis on the correct amount of detail during this stage of the design effort is also to minimize the disruptive effect of meetings with the operating personnel. It is difficult to specify a hard and fast rule because the complexities of the system are the main criteria. A guide for determining the amount of detail required is that there should be enough information in the documentation so that a person unfamiliar with the application can obtain a thorough under-

INFORMATION TO BE DOCUMENTED	REASON FOR INFORMATION
1. Location which operations take place	Information regarding physical locations is needed: a. to determine locations at which terminals can/may be placed b. along with items 5, 6 and 7 below, to determine duplication of efforts at other locations within the company
2. Person(s) performing the action	Supplies information as to: a. who requires access to terminals b. whose method of performing work will be changed
3. a. The type and number of Input Records to the action b. The type and number of Output Records from the action	The type and quantity of Input-Output transactions that will be going to – from the computer
4. Files – file records used	Required for determining auxiliary storage requirements
5. Action taken and why it is done (ex. calls storeroom. Why? To determine if item is in stock.) a. Normal condition b. Emergency condition c. Special (error condition)	Needed for the development of real-time operational program logic
6. Previous Action	Needed for the development of real-time operational program logic
7. Subsequent Action	Needed for the development of real-time operational program logic
8. Problems occurring during (because of) performance of assigned duties	Needed for the development of real-time operational program logic

Figure 3.3

standing of present operations. The greater the complexity, of course, the greater the detail. There should be enough information so that the system could be designed by a qualified person even though he has never visited any of the operating departments.

Details are of greater importance in designing a real-time system than in designing a batch type system for the following reasons:

1. Real-time systems combine different types of equipment, each interacting in closely timed coordination.
2. There is a greater chance for miscalculations. Even minor omissions and errors can result in a nonworkable system. It is therefore important that, prior to the beginning of the implementation effort, there be as much assurance as possible that the system will function as required by management.
3. The implementation team will be writing and testing routines that, though programmed separately, must work together. The programming of routines that will function in such an environment, that is, real-time, requires that they be specified in great detail. The amount of detail required must therefore be dictated by those who will be designing and implementing the new system.

The requirements of the new system together with complexity of the presently existing system determine the level of detail to be maintained by those analyzing existing procedures.

Training the study-team members

Once the study team is fully staffed (for this phase) the study-team manager must be sure that each team member knows what must be obtained, how he goes about getting it (where it can be found), and how to document his findings. Their training should consist of a series of lectures. A formalized approach is a more efficient and expeditious way of teaching to everyone what is demanded and expected. Each lesson should be discussed, permitting problems and answers to be dissected by the team members.

The agenda for these sessions should include the following:

1. (a) A review of the company, its history, products, present objectives, as well as its future goals.
   (b) Management's anticipation of the benefits to be obtained from the real-time system.
   (c) A review of the organization of the company. The real-time system must be a company-wide effort even though it is being

designed and implemented by specialists. For this reason, plus the fact that it is always best to get the most accurate information, a manager from each of the departments (or divisions) to be studied should present his department's organization, method of accomplishing its functions, and its problems.

2. Information to be obtained from the operating departments and why it is needed.
3. The techniques used for obtaining information from the operating department, that is, the methods of conducting interviews.
4. Documentation standards. This includes what information is to be documented as well as the amount of detail required.

To ensure that the material covered is retained, each analyst should receive a folder containing outlines of the material covered in these classes. The forms that are to be used by the analysts should also be included in the folder. These together with the notes taken during class should be reviewed by the analyst when working with the operating departments.

Making work assignments

On completion of formal training, the study-team members should be given their work assignments. An assignment should include

(a) a copy of the scope of the study, as specified by the steering committee,
(b) the application that the study-team member is to analyze,
(c) the department(s) he will be studying,
(d) who the initial contact is in the department—that is, the person who will coordinate and be responsible for instructing and showing the analyst all information necessary for the study,
(e) the data on which the study of present procedures are to be completed,
(f) the date of the first progress meeting (At this meeting the study-team manager will review the progress of the analyst as well as problems he has encountered),
(g) designation of additional person or persons from the operating departments to be assigned to work with the analyst during his study of present procedures.

It is rare to find one person with experience in the two areas required, namely a thorough understanding of automated data processing and comprehensive knowledge of the manner in which information is presently processed by the operating department(s). Depending on the previous experience of the study-team members, there are several possibilities available to the team manager:

(a) Assigning two persons to each application/department, one with a data processing background, and the other with experience in the present system,

(b) Assigning one person with data processing experience, relying on his ability and training and the cooperation of the operating department's personnel.

(c) Assigning three analysts to each application/department. Although they will work together during the study of the existing procedures, each will submit his own design of the flow and processing for the new system. The study-team manager, on review of the three new system designs will choose those parts of each that, in his opinion, will constitute the best over-all design. This approach, although more expensive, offers a greater possibility for a successful design than the others.

No matter which approach the study-team manager finally chooses, the most experienced personnel should be assigned to the more complicated and/or important applications.

ANALYSIS OF PRESENT OPERATIONS

There are basically two ways in which information concerning existing procedures can be obtained—reading and interviewing. Reading procedural manuals as well as operating instructions and guides can provide the systems analyst with much important information. Unfortunately, these documents become obsolete, especially in a growing organization, in a short period of time, and they often do not contain the level of detail required, since they are guides for the existing operations, not an input for real-time systems design.

Interviewing company personnel and observing the methods used throughout the departments under study provide a fruitful source of information. Depending on the attitude of the personnel being interviewed, obtaining information can be a difficult task. Unless full cooperation is obtained the people being interviewed will provide only the information requested, volunteering little. Developing a rapport, making them feel a part of the new system, and reassuring them that they will not be replaced by the new system must all be accomplished by the interviewer. Upper management can (and must) help, but in the end, the systems analyst must *sell* himself, the new system, and the study in order to obtain the information he requires. Obtaining procedural information from operating personnel requires that the systems analyst *ask the right question, listen,* and *observe.* This is particularly important since, most of the time, the people being interviewed do not know what information the analyst needs. The analyst must therefore learn how to interview; to ask questions.

The following are some sample questions which may be used by the systems analyst for guiding the interview. The interviewee's response, after each statement cannot be exactly assumed, therefore it has not been included.

Start—Introductions

I understand that you are responsible for _____

Does this mean that you get (do) _____ forms _____ from _____

Do you have to process many different kinds of transactions?

Can you give me a sample of each?

Why? I'd like to see if *we* can combine or eliminate forms so that your work can be made easier, especially during rush hours.

How many do you get?

Is this number constant, or does it fluctuate?

Taking, or talking about the first form, what do you do with it? (Do you have to go to any files?)

What do you do with it after you're finished with it?

Is any of this information needed as a permanent record?

Is any special handling or processing ever required? What do you do?

Are there any standard procedures for taking care of these special conditions/exceptions?

(This information is gathered for all forms.)

Can changes or requests be made by telephone . . . or special memo? (If yes) Who makes the request/change and how is it done?

Should an unforseen snag arise; for example, an error is suspected or apparent in a document, what is done about it?

DOCUMENTATION FOR SUBSEQUENT ANALYSIS

During the interview the analyst should take only the briefest notes to allow for minimum interruptions to the conversation. At the end of *each* day the analyst should document in detail, while it is still fresh in his mind. This information, when completed, will be reviewed by

(a) the department personnel (management from whom the information was obtained) for correctness,
(b) the study-team manager for completeness,
(c) the steering committee, during various phases of the study as well as when the final study report is submitted.

The use to which this information will be put provides the key to how it should be documented. Information concerning existing procedures will be collected application by application for the next phase of the project. This documentation is the source of information for the specification of the operational program logic, input and output messages, files, terminals, and line and line control unit(s) of the new system. The information should be reorganized in a manner shown schematically in Figure 3.4. The relationship of this documentation in terms of the total system design effort is shown in Figure 3.5.

Using the future uses of the documentation of existing procedures as a guide, several rules can be applied to the specification for documentation standards. The documentation should:

1. Be organized in a manner that, regardless of the level of detail, the user
   (a) will be readily able to find the level in which he is interested,
   (b) can fulfill his requirements with a minimum of "page jumping" (i.e. the same detail level collated in sequence).
2. Be easy to cross-reference and reorganize.
3. Insist that each type document be of the same format.

For these reasons, preprinted forms are recommended. Preprinted forms, are numerous in type as well as format (see Figures 3.6, 3.7, and 3.8).

Figure 3.6 is an example of an IBM–SOP File Sheet which contains information relating to one file.[2] On one sheet are listed 18 different fields. This one sheet contains all the information required for a file to be converted and used as a part of a real-time system.

[2] Reprinted by permission from IBM. SOP, Study Organization Plan—see IBM Manual No. C20-8075 entitled "IBM Study Organization Plan—Documentation Techniques," © 1961 International Business Machines Corporation.

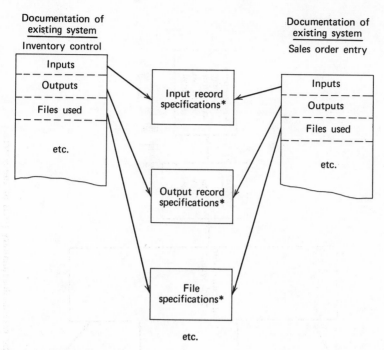

Figure 3.4 The items with asterisks can be *completed* only after the analysis of existing procedures.

Figure 3.7, a Procedure Analysis Form,[3] provides on one sheet room for information concerning Input-Output documents, the flow of information, processes and remarks. Figure 3.8, a Flow Process Chart,[4] is useful for detailing physical actions and distances interrelated with the data processing function. A review of the various fields in each of the forms indicates the types of information that will be needed. Depending upon the complexity of the application, all three forms could be used—if they were properly cross referenced. It is left to the discretion of the study-team manager whether he will use existing formats or will utilize sections of various forms developing a customized set of documents for the system design effort.

The documentation of each application should be completed in duplicate, one set to be kept for reference becoming a part of the final

[3] Reproduced from *Management Standards for Data Processing*, Brandon, R, Van Nostrand Reinhold Company, New York, 1963, p. 52.

[4] Nelson, Oscar and Richard Woods, *Accounting Systems and Data Processing*, South-Western Publishing Company, Cincinnati, Ohio, 1961, p. 224.

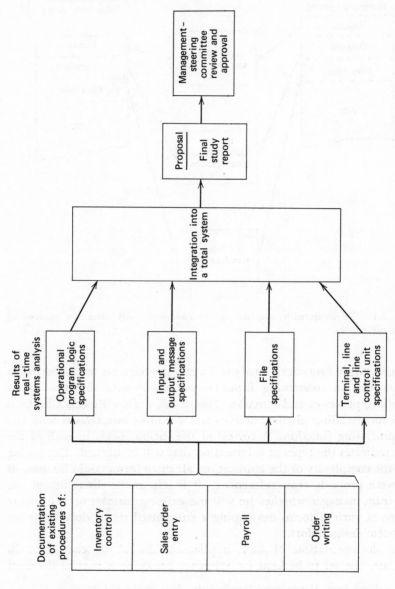

Figure 3.5 Schematic of the uses of the various documentary parts of the system.

study report. The other to be reorganized becoming the working source document for the design of the new system. Complete documentation of an application should contain the following 12 sections:

1. Cover page—consisting of name of application, departments studied, dates of studies, and names and signatures of the analyst, the project manager, and the operating departmental managers (to show their concurrence with the findings and problems of the application report).
2. Table of contents.
3. Copies of the scope of the study of each application.
4. Organization chart of the departments involved and the application being studied.
5. Narrative of the data flow. (This general 2- to 4-page, high-level application/description should be supplemented by a schematic of the data flow across the various departments.)
6. List of major problem areas—those concerned with these problems and recommended solutions (if any).
7. Minutes of all meetings documented in narrative form, including all agreements and conclusions as well as what was discussed.
8. Floor plan of each department.
9. Symbolic flow diagram of all information-processing within detailed descriptions of each step of the flow.
10. File data—detailed information concerning all files.
11. Transactions formats—data concerning inputs and outputs relating to this application (cross referenced to section 12).
12. Transaction volumes—information concerning the number of transactions occurring at various intervals.

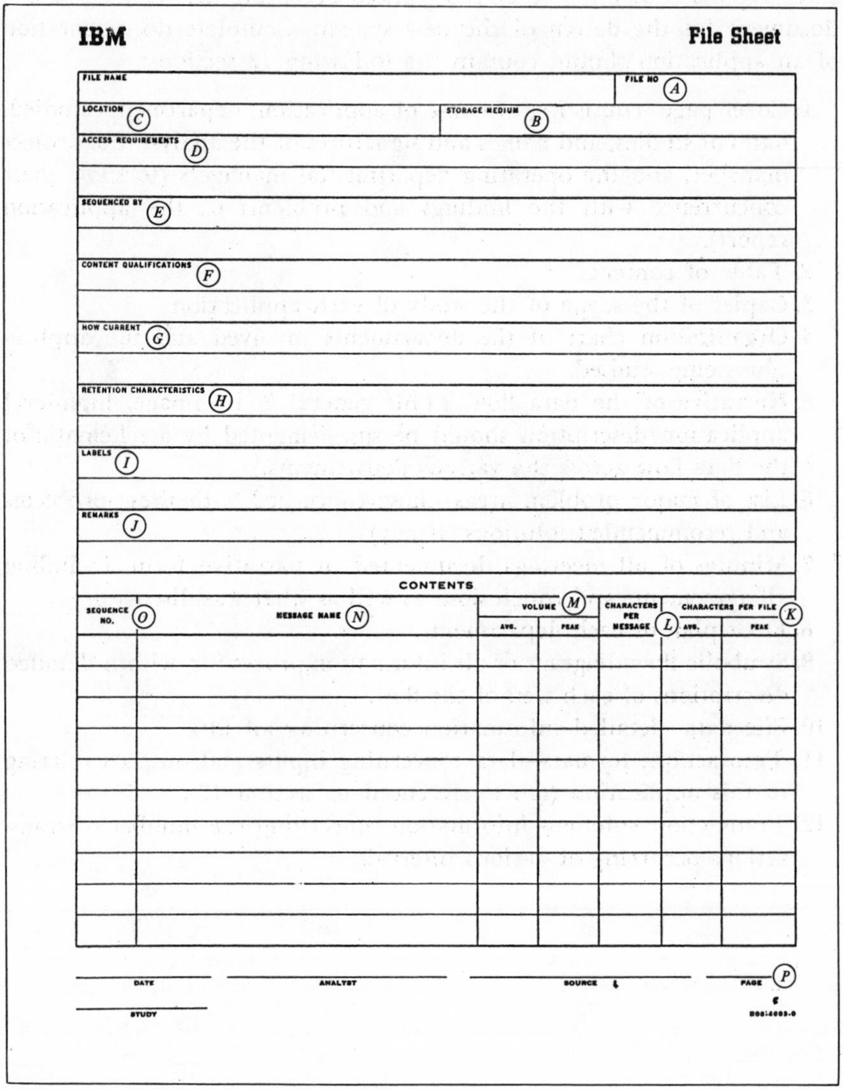
IBM **File Sheet**

FILE NAME | FILE NO (A)

LOCATION (C) | STORAGE MEDIUM (B)

ACCESS REQUIREMENTS (D)

SEQUENCED BY (E)

CONTENT QUALIFICATIONS (F)

HOW CURRENT (G)

RETENTION CHARACTERISTICS (H)

LABELS (I)

REMARKS (J)

CONTENTS

SEQUENCE NO. (O)	MESSAGE NAME (N)	VOLUME (M)		CHARACTERS PER MESSAGE (L)	CHARACTERS PER FILE (K)	
		AVG.	PEAK		AVG.	PEAK

DATE | ANALYST | SOURCE | PAGE (P)

STUDY

Figure 3.6

A. An analyst assignment number used for referencing the file during subsequent stages of the project.

B. Indicates how the data are presently stored—in a file cabinet, on tape, on punched cards, etc.

C. Where the information is located.

D. What information is needed to find a specific record—customer number, name of vendor, part number, etc.

E. The sequence in which the file is maintained.

F. The criteria that are used to determine if an entry is to be placed on the file (or maintained), e.g., an active client, a presently used part number.

G. How often the file is updated and/or purged.

H. How long a record can remain in the file before being purged, e.g., stays in the file if there has been activity within the last 18 months.

I. Only applicable if the file is stored in tape.

J. Miscellaneous relevant comments and information.

K. The average and maximum number of characters updated when processing this message.

L. The number of characters in the message (message length).

M. Average and peak number of transactions accessing this file.

N. The name or identification of the transactions accessing this file.

O. Sequential numbering of all messages.

P. Information identifying the source of the above, who produced it, when it was done and to which part of the study it is related.

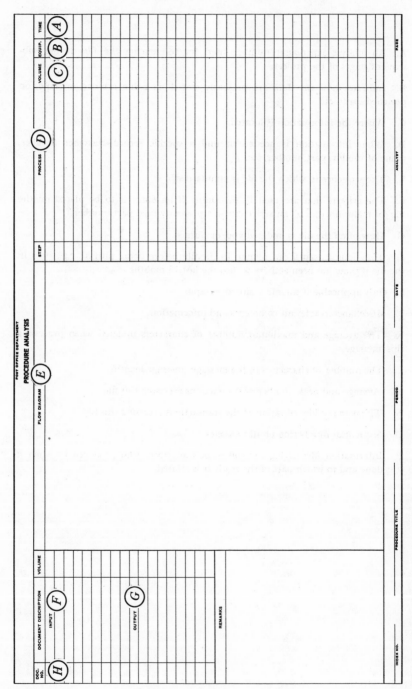

Figure 3.7 (Courtesy of the Post Office Department)

A. Estimated processing time for each of the transactions listed in F. and G.

B. Equipment to be used—card reader, paper tape, printer, etc.—for each of the transactions listed in F and G.

C. Number of transactions for each of the inputs/outputs listed in F and G.

D. Description of the processing.

E. High-level flow diagram.

F. List of input messages for this application.

G. List of output messages for this application.

H. Reference number cross referencing to a more detailed layout of the input/output message.

Job: Processing Receiving Aprons	☑ Procedure ☐ Form	☐ Individual ☐ Other	Page 1 of 1
	Charted by A. Smith		Date 3/10/6–

Step No.	Operation	Transportation	Inspection	Storage	Details of Present Method	Distance	Quantity	Analysis
1	◯	◯	☐	▽	**Receiver** Receives merchandise and signs freight bills			
2	◯	◯	☐	▽	Records data on master sheet and apron			
3	◯	◯	☐	▽	Attaches invoice or packing slip to apron			
4	◯	◯	☐	▽	Attaches apron to merchandise			
5	◯	◯	☐	▽	**Stock Boy** Transfers merchandise and aprons to mdse. checking area	100 ft.		
6	◯	◯	☐	▽	Stores merchandise and aprons in mdse. checking area			
7	◯	◯	☐	▽	**Merchandise Checker** Removes aprons from merchandise			
8	◯	◯	☐	▽	Checks number of packages against apron			
9	◯	◯	☐	▽	Opens packages			
10	◯	◯	☐	▽	Lists items and quantities on apron			
11	◯	◯	☐	▽	Tickets mdse. for apron number			
12	◯	◯	☐	▽	Files documents awaiting transport			
13	◯	◯	☐	▽	**Runner** (3 times daily) Transports aprons to accounts payable	500 yds		
14	◯	◯	☐	▽	**Receiver** Files completed master sheets in box			
15	◯	◯	☐	▽				

Figure 3.8

CONCLUSION

Gathering the information used in the design of a real-time system, begins with the study of present procedures. The steps involved can be summarized as follows:

1. Make initial preparations by
   (a) contacting and establishing lines of communication with the operating departments which will be involved with the applications to be studied,
   (b) specifying documentation requirements,
   (c) training the study-team members, and
   (d) making work assignments.
2. Analyze the company's present operating procedures.
3. Document all information obtained from the operating departments in accordance with the previously defined documentation requirements.

The review and approval of the documentation of present procedures completes this part of the study.

CHAPTER 4

Determining System Performance Requirements

DESIGNING A REAL-TIME SYSTEM REQUIRES THE SPECIFICATION OF THE TASKS TO BE ACCOMPLISHED. DETERMINING SYSTEM PERFORMANCE REQUIREMENTS INVOLVES ASCERTAINING THE NUMBER OF TRANSACTIONS THAT THE COMPUTER MUST ACCEPT, PROCESS, AND RETURN TO THE TERMINAL OPERATOR. THE STEPS INVOLVED IN DETERMINING THE NUMBER OF EXPECTED TRANSACTIONS ARE ANALYZED IN THIS CHAPTER.

An important performance capability of a real-time system is its ability to reduce time delays. The prompt acceptance of transactions whenever they are entered into the system from terminal locations, with neither intermediate handling nor delays, reduces the time span from input through processing to output. Receiving inputs and returning processed outputs on this basis necessitates the acceptance of transactions, by the computer, whose time and rate of entry is controlled by the terminal operator. It is this removal of control—that is, the capability of deciding when to accept inputs from the computer to the terminal operator, combined with the ability of the system to accept inputs of all types (in any sequence) and the immediate outputting of the processed transactions, that directly influences the size and speed of the central processing unit.

The effect that this requirement of immediate acceptance, processing and return to the terminal operator can have upon a real-time system is shown in Figures 4.1a through d. Each chart illustrates different rates of transactions entering and leaving the system. All four, however, portray the same average number (sum) of inputs and outputs for one transaction type to be processed by the system. Each is plotted with a time scale on the x axis versus transaction volumes on the y axis. The time scale of each spans an equivalent time period of the "real-time day." The charts are the "electrocardiograph" of the real-time system in that they show fluctuations as they occur with the passage of time.

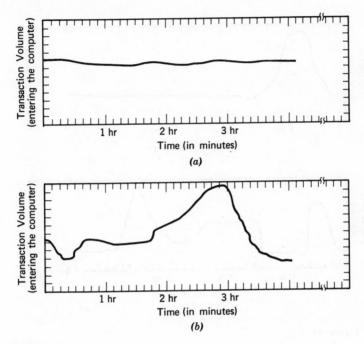

Figure 4.1

Figure 4.1a presents the sum of transactions coming into and leaving the system at a rate similar to that of a batch type system. The slope is basically level because the inputs are evenly spaced throughout the real-time day. The transaction volumes in Figures 4.1b, 4.1c, and 4.1d can vary because

(a) of the uncontrollable rate of input of the various transactions, from remote locations, which in turn cause a fluctuation in the rate of processing required during the real-time day, and

(b) of messages coming into the system *simultaneously* for many locations.

It is not uncommon in a real-time system for transactions to be received by the computer in the manner illustrated in Figures 4.1b, 4.1c and 4.1d. It should be noted that, while the volume of transactions shown in these examples is level in slope, the number of messages entering and leaving the system in any given period of time may not be constant as shown, but could be cyclic, decreasing or increasing.

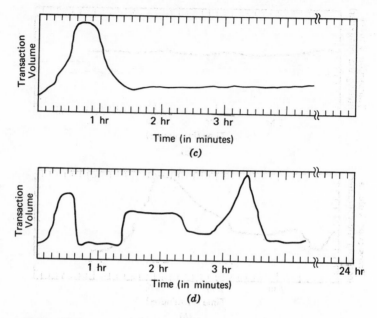

Figure 4.1

The system analyst must determine the time, duration, and extent of the fluctuation for *each* type of transaction. It is the estimated time interval that the greatest number of messages will be entering and leaving the system that determines the transaction processing requirements of the system. The maximum number of transactions that can be expected to enter and to leave the system in a designated time interval is called the peak period. The system analyst has to determine when the peak period will take place and ascertain the manner in which the peak period is developed. As the computer size is affected by the peak number of transactions, it is therefore, important to determine the characteristics of this peak (or peaks since there can be several). The system that can process these maximums will naturally be able to process any lesser number of transactions, those occurring during nonpeak periods.

Expanding the previous example, the effect that *two* types of messages can have on a system are shown in Figure 4.2. Message type *A* has minimal fluctuations. Message type *B* fluctuates radically. (In this example, the averages for both messages are also the same.) If the

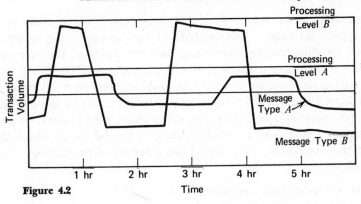

Figure 4.2

computer has only to process, during the peak period, messages of type *A*, it would have to maintain a processing level (thruput) shown as Processing Level *A*. Fluctuations of the type shown for message type *B* require, all other things being equal, a computer capable of maintaining a higher processing level, processing level *B*. A more powerful computer would therefore be required. In order to be able to process *both* types concurrently, a computer able to process the sum of the transaction volumes (the sum of processing levels *A*, and *B*) would be required. In a fully operational real-time system, the number of message types may be as many as several score, each with different slopes and each requiring a different amount of processing during one or more peak periods. One can begin to see the complexities involved when specifying system thruput requirements for such an operating environment. The best method for developing system performance requirements is to follow a set of pre-specified procedures. A system analyst, in order to determine the processing level, the peak period(s), and the number of transactions the real time system must be able to process should proceed as follows:

1. Define and list all transactions types.
2. Determine peak periods for all transactions.
3. Project all peak periods.
4. Determine over-all level of thruput.

DEFINE AND LIST ALL TRANSACTION TYPES

A list of transaction types for each application must be developed first. A review of presently existing procedures as well as analysis of scope of the real-time system are sources for this information. The review of the existing procedures will supply data concerning present transactions types and rates. The analysis of the scope of the study, as developed by the steering committee, and the goals of the company, as specified by management, together with an understanding of the types of information that can be produced by real-time systems form the basis for ascertaining the types of transactions to be processed by the real-time system. For example, a real-time sales order entry system would be processing customer orders on a real-time basis. A partial list of transaction types for this application developed from a review of the message sheets is the following:

1. Enter an order (old customer).
2. Enter an order (new customer).
3. Eliminate an order that was previously entered.
4. Change customer's billing name and/or address.
5. Change ship-to-name and/or address.
6. Modify delivery date(s).
7. Change terms of payment.
8. Correct unit price.
9. Change quantity requested.
10. Add an item to an order.
11. Delete an item from an order.
12. Credit the customer's account.

These transactions occur in the presently existing system. If the documentation of existing procedures is properly detailed, the list will also include those transactions which are verbal in nature (e.g., telephone calls) as well as those which are memos or written on scraps of paper (both are applicable to real-time processing).

To this list of existing transactions must be added all new transaction types. New transactions come into being because real-time systems are capable of making available information which has been stored either in a sequence other than that maintained at present or summarized from part(s) of one or more files of data.

Records and data that were formerly unavailable to various operating personnel because of cost and/or time required for preparation represent the major type of such new transactions. Referring to the sales order entry application, for instance, some of this new information consists of

(a) determining a customer's purchases over a given period.
(b) determining how much all customers have bought of product z this month compared to last month.

(c) the customer's record of payments over the last x months.

(d) the customer's record of purchases over the last x months.

A review of the information to be stored on auxiliary storage is also a source for additional transaction types. Any data stored on auxiliary storage can be made available to interested parties. Until the files have been specified, such a list should be considered to be preliminary in nature.

As management and operating personnel realize the types of information that the real-time system makes available to them, they will request all sorts of additional information from it. Thus, the addition of new transaction types as well as changes to the number of transactions often continues until the beginning of system implementation, or until such time as no additional changes are permitted. New additions can have a major impact upon the entire system. The addition of any transaction types coming into the system *during the peak period* will cause additional utilization of components that are already working at a high level. Because of this, system performance requirements cannot be considered to be fully completed, until all transaction types have been determined. Once approved, these new transaction types plus the existing message types become a list of the transactions that the system must be able to accept, process, and route. This list will be used as a basis for the development of further information.

DETERMINE PEAK PERIODS FOR ALL TRANSACTIONS

It is the peak period that will cause the highest utilization of one or more system components for a varying period of real-time. It is mainly during peak period(s) that delays could occur. These delays cause an increase in the time required to process a transaction and then send it (the updated message) to its destination. The delays are caused by transactions entering the system at a more rapid rate than they can be processed. The system analyst's job is to ensure that such delays, if they do occur, take place as infrequently as possible, and that they will be of minimum duration.

The system analyst must continuously review his work to be sure that there is minimal deviation between his estimates and the actual number of transactions. Since he will be working with considerable data, it is advisable to categorize these first into scheduled and random transmissions, then concentrate on those intervals containing the larger number of random transmissions.

Scheduled transmissions

Depending upon the requirements of the application, there are transactions which can be saved (batched) and forwarded from various locations to the computer in a steady stream. For instance, payroll data can be transferred to the computer for processing in this manner. All variable payroll information can be entered into the system via the terminals at each location. These data can be batched and transferred in a continuous stream, one transaction immediately following another. The time of day the data are to be transferred should be specified to take place during non-peak periods, since an *immediate response* is not required. (An immediate response is defined as one in which information is returned as output, within moments (seconds to minutes) of the receipt of input.) Batching of payroll transactions, for example, can be tolerated if the delay caused by batching of the input does not reduce its timeliness. As long as the data (the checks) arrive on or before the time required, such batching of transactions is permissable. Whenever possible the system analyst should recommend the time of day of all scheduled transactions for other than peak periods. By allocating the processing of scheduled transmissions in this manner the analyst can concentrate on determining those messages whose time of entry and processing cannot be scheduled or shifted—that is, the random transmissions.

Random transmissions

Whenever data are needed on an immediate response basis, transaction turn-around time (the time when the transaction is sent into the system until it is fully processed and forwarded to its destination) must be reduced to a *reasonable* interval of time. (As will be shown subsequently "reasonableness" is a managerial decision.) Information must appear where it is needed and when it is required. The technique used by the computer system for reducing delays under these conditions is to receive and process transactions whenever the information is needed by the terminal operator. Whenever a transaction requires an immediate response, techniques must be introduced to minimize the time span from input to output. This means that the computer system must either be able to process transactions as they are received regardless of the application, or temporarily store messages on auxiliary storage, provided the latter (called queuing) will not create "unreasonable delays." This forwarding of a transaction for processing with *no* restrictions on the order in which the transaction must enter the system is called a random transmission.

To determine into which classification (scheduled or random) a transaction should be assigned, the following question should be posed. Does the time delay required for batching or queuing a transaction before processing by the system create problems (within the company) that can be avoided by the reduction of time interval between entry of the transaction into the computer and receipt of a response? If the answer is yes, the transaction should be classified as a random transmission. There is an exception, in that there are transactions that would be specified as random transmissions although they could be "batched." They would not be batched because they are comparatively few in number. For example, payroll information relating to recent hires, layoffs, etc. Again, schedulable transmissions should be fixed for other than peak periods.

The system analyst should now concentrate on developing information regarding the maximum number of random transmissions that can be expected. Information relating to existing message types can be developed from the information obtained from the study of existing procedures. Information involving new transaction types will consist mainly of estimates based on the volume of existing related transactions; for example, the transaction that is concerned with the status of an order. How many telephone calls, letters, and internal requests for information of this type have been made in the past? It is true that the resulting transaction volume estimates may be inaccurate, but by planning for feedback statistics, a higher degree of accuracy can be developed.

Before proceeding, the system analyst must determine if there are any corporate plans (reorganizations, acquisitions, mergers, etc.) which could affect, upward or downward, the number of transactions that the system must process. A positive response would necessitate adjustments to the information gathered to date, reflecting the changes in transaction volumes caused by various corporate initiatives.

Once transactions have been categorized into scheduled and random, the following steps can be followed to determine when the peak periods will occur and which transactions will be processed during these intervals:

1. Summarize the number of transactions by month for enough periods to extract information concerning trend and peak month for *each* of the random transactions. (A statistician should specify the number of periods for the first try.)
2. Have these summarized totals examined by the statistician, so that a

statistically valid trend can be determined. To find the peak periods, the trend of transaction volume must be determined. There are four types of possible trends—constant, increasing, decreasing, and cyclic. For those transactions which show no trend, but for which there is reason to believe that a trend exists, more data must be analyzed. This can consist of adjusting the span time for which the transactions have been summarized (such as from a month to a day—from a day to an hour) or the initiation of a sampling plan. Whatever the procedures recommended, they must be followed until statistically valid trends have been developed for *each* random transmission.

3. Analyze the data to determine the peak period of the *current* year. The weeks of the month specified as peak should be compared with the same week(s) of the previous year, as the statistician will be looking for a recurring pattern. Points *A* and *B* of Figure 4.3 illustrate such a pattern.

The list of transaction volumes occurring during the peak week is then analyzed to determine the peak day(s) as well as the number of transactions that take place during these times.

Utilizing a list of peak day(s) for each transaction type, the system analyst must

(a) determine the peak hours and the peak minutes [1] within those hours.

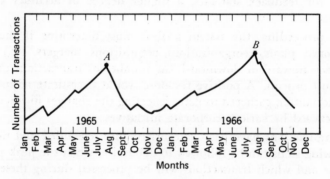

Figure 4.3

---

[1] It may seem that determination of peak minutes is unnecessary delving into too minute detail. However, considering the fact that computers work in millionths and billionths of a second, transactions per minute encompass a long span of processing time.

(b) hypothesize, if possible, the shape of the transaction's peak (how quickly the peak builds up) and specify procedures to enable a count (with time of occurrence) of these transactions the next time the peak period is taking place.[2]

At this point the system analyst should have developed, for each transaction type, the following information:

1. The number of transactions occurring during the peak period.
2. The time duration of the peak.
3. The rate of change (trend) that has taken place until the present.

This information can be obtained from the study of existing procedures as well as from four major sources/techniques. These are

(a) querying experienced personnel.
(b) relative weighing of transaction types.
(c) analysis of historical data.
(d) initiation of sampling plans.

Querying experienced personnel. The quickest way of determining peak periods is to ask concerned personnel. In most organizations there are personnel who, because of their experience, can tell the system designer when peak periods have been taking place. This information can be a guide for a first analysis of transaction volumes.

Relative weighing of transaction types. The specification of operational program logic permits the system designer to develop an estimate of the time required to process each transaction. As this information may not yet be available, the specifications of the operational programs, once developed, should be reviewed to ensure that there are no additional peak periods as the ones now being described. A list of processing estimates using the execution times for the machine specified as the CPU will show the relative processing requirements of each transaction type. Figure 4.4 lists estimated processing time for four transaction types. "Enter an order—new customer" is estimated to take 17 times as long to process as the transaction "Determine customer's credit limit."

A new order entry, being a more time consuming transaction, assumes a higher relative weight. Those transactions possessing a high weight require a more careful analysis. The adverse effect on a real-time system of a miscalculation in a highly weighted transaction type is

[2] There is an assumption implied which should be validated, that peaks will occur with the same frequency and duration as in the past.

Transaction Type	Estimated Execution Time
1. Enter an order -- new customer	1,750 ms (milleseconds)
2. Changed terms of payment	420 ms
3. Delete an item from an order	850 ms
4. Determine customer's credit limit	100 ms

Figure 4.4

naturally greater than with a type having a low relative weight. For example, an estimate of 3,000 new customer order entries compared with an actual number of 3480 of these transactions would cause greater system problems than an equivalent wrong estimate of the number of transactions for "Determine customer's credit limit." Therefore, the peak volume with the largest number of highly weighted processing types must be watched as closely as the peak with the greatest number of transactions. The higher the relative rating, the greater the degree of attention must be accorded to the transaction type.

Analysis of historical data. Many business firms have records that can be made available for examination. These records contain information about past activity regarding various transaction types. This information should be reviewed to see if it incorporates desired statistical information, that is if it is recorded in meaningful time intervals. (A report with only yearly summarizations, for example, will be of minimal use.) Analysis of historical data can require correlation of hundreds of thousands of records. This activity done manually can be time consuming as the data needs to be summarized into many different categories. Fortunately, computerized routines, data-reduction programs, are available or can be written to reduce this workload. Once historical data is translated into machine intelligible form, a data reduction program can be run as often as desired to obtain various categories of information.[3] The number of occurrences can be categorized into any time period along with the percentage of occurrence in each category and cumulative percentage for the same transaction. As control cards

[3] E.g. IBM's DARS—Data Reduction System.

are used to specify the sort, the count fields and the desired time span, the peak month, can quickly and accurately be determined. The report can then be run analyzing only the peak month, thus homing in on when the peak period occurs for each transaction type. The effort and cost required to produce such reports for each transaction type, manually, would make such a detailed analysis prohibitive.

Initiation of sampling plans. A sampling plan can be instituted for those transactions which

(a) have no historical data available,
(b) defy the development of statistically valid results, or
(c) require a more detailed study of the peak period.

It is important that a statistician be consulted for the implementation of any sampling plan since he can determine the minimum data required to obtain the needed information. He must also be available for the statistically correct interpretation of samples and summarized data.

PROJECT ALL PEAK PERIODS

In order to ascertain how far all trends are to be projected the system analyst must obtain from management an answer to the question: For what time period must the equipment that is being specified be able to process the real-time input without any change (additions or deletions) to the equipment selected—that is, addition of more auxiliary storage units, more core storage, etc?

All trends will be extended to the date which management specifies. If this extension represents a rapid rate of increase instead of specifying a system capable of processing the entire volume, a shorter target can be used in combination with the development of a schedule of delivery of equipment for handling the higher volume. Now that the systems analyst knows how many transactions will be occurring during the peak period he must next determine the response time (called answerback) desired by management.

DETERMINE THE OVER-ALL LEVEL OF THRUPUT

The over-all level of thruput (called the systems benchmark) is a processing and response time specification which, in the opinion of management, must be maintained during peak periods by the real-time system. To the systems analyst, this represents a definite goal. Remember that the benchmark is a performance level which the computer system *must* be able to meet, and if it cannot, it must be considered an unacceptable system. The performance requirements are often specified as x number of transactions per (min/sec/hour) with a response time of y, z percent of the time. The summarization of the various transaction types that occur at the same time are represented by x, and z percent of the time is a statistical confidence level. In the following example there are three transaction types that make up the peak hour.

Transaction Type	Number of Transactions occurring during peak hour
New Customer Order	176
Old Customer Order	82
Request for Customer Credit Limit	94
	352

Based on an even distribution during the peak hour, the system would be required to process 352/60 or 5.8 transactions per minute. Given a response time requirements of two minutes, the resulting performance requirement is that the system must be able to process 5.8 transactions per minute with a response time of two minutes or less 95% of the time. Ninety-five percent is a confidence level determined by a statistician. This means that, based on statistically valid calculations and the assumptions specified, no more than 5 percent of the time will this response time of two minutes be exceeded. This number, and the transaction volumes it represents is the key to the processing capability required by the system.

It is the responsibility of the system designer to document all assumptions as well as all information developed in this phase of the study. Included must be decisions based on statistically valid data. At all times, the systems analyst must remember that there must be substantiation of all his decisions and justification for his conclusions.

CONCLUSION

The maximum number of transactions that the real-time system will have to process (called the system benchmark) is developed as follows:

1. List all transactions that will be entering the system—regardless of type.
2. Divide all transactions into scheduled and nonscheduled (random) transmissions.

3. For all random transmissions

(a) determine peak period,
(b) ascertain from management the number of years that the system must be able to process transactions without changing the configuration.
(c) determine the trend of each of the transactions occurring during the peak period,
(d) project all trends until the year ascertained in step 3b,
(e) check for weighted peak periods, and
(f) review all work with a statistician.

4. Assign all scheduled transactions for other than peak periods.
5. Determine the systems benchmark.
6. Document all analysis and assumptions.
7. Submit the documentation to the steering committee for approval.

CHAPTER 5

Specifying the Central Processing Unit(s)

I. CONCEPTS AND TERMS*

New technology gives rise to new concepts and new terms and thus a higher level of sophistication. Computer hardware with its accompanying programming systems make possible the efficient application of a real-time system for the modern and sophisticated demands of industry. Both the developed state of the art of computer components and their program systems are indivisible and interdependent parts of the whole real-time system. Prior to the introduction of real-time data processing, most computer systems were limited to

(a) fully processing one transaction before being able to begin the next,

(b) a general level of programming support supplied by computer manufacturers, which consisted mainly of compilers and routines servicing tapes, disks, card readers, punches, and printers,

(c) one level of hardware interrupt (completion of a tape or disk operation) end of form on the printer, was provided by computer circuitry.

Figure 5.1 is a diagrammatic sample of the sequence of permissible operations in such an environment.

Because of the differential in the operating speed between the computer and the various auxiliary units, a large percentage of the time required to process a transaction was wasted in awaiting the completion of an Input-Output operation. In order to gain a more efficient utiliza-

---

* Real-time systems represent an advanced method of processing data. In order to familiarize the reader with some of these new concepts and terms this, and several of the chapters that follow have been divided into two sections. The first, labeled Concepts and Terms, provides basic background. The second, uses that information discussed in Section I as the basis for that phase of system design.

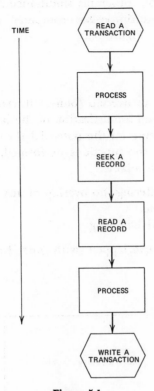

TIME

READ A TRANSACTION

PROCESS

SEEK A RECORD

READ A RECORD

PROCESS

WRITE A TRANSACTION

Figure 5.1

tion of the data processing equipment and consequently an increase in the number of transactions processed in a given period of time, new designs and their techniques were introduced. The major data processing innovations of importance in the design of a real-time system are

    (a) multiprocessing
    (b) buffering capability
    (c) multiprogramming
    (d) reentrant programming.

MULTIPROCESSING

Multiprocessing is the capability of a single central processing unit (CPU) to execute more than one instruction at the same time. The capabilities of such a system can be compared to one in which several computers process one or more programs simultaneously. A schematic representation of a (one) multiprocessor computer sharing a single common memory is shown in Figure 5.2.

BUFFERING CAPABILITY

The ability of a computer to overlap (buffer) internal functions has been made possible by increased sophistication of the internal circuitry.[1] This ability has a direct bearing on the potential thruput of a system. As related to overlapping of the functions performed, there are three distinct classes of computers available.

1. Computers having no buffering—no overlap of any input or output with processing is possible.
2. Computers having partial buffering

   (a) processing can be overlapped with *one* Input or Output operation,[2] or

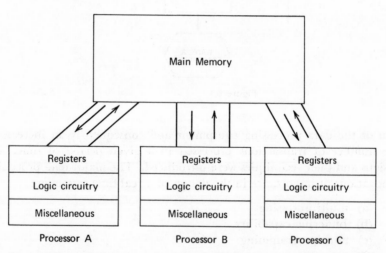

Processor A Processor B Processor C

Figure 5.2 Block diagram of a computor having multiprocessing capability.

[1] Buffering is the capability of a computer to perform in parallel input-output operation(s) with processing.

[2] It should be noted that whenever processing is overlapped with I–O, processing time is slightly increased due to cycle stealing—that is, a part of each instruction execution is delayed to permit a unit of data to be transferred from or to, the control unit into, or from, main computer memory.

(b) an Input-Output operation can be overlapped with another Input-Output operation but not with processing.

3. Computers having full buffering—Input and Output operations can be overlapped with each other *and* with processing.

Assuming full buffering capabilities, the extent that this sophistication of computer hardware can affect transaction processing is illustrated as follows. Using the sequence of operations shown in Figure 5.1 as a reference, assume four similar transactions are queued in computer memory ready for simultaneous processing. Each has the following flow and timing requirements:

First:	10 ms (milliseconds) processing
Second:	60 ms seek disk record
Third:	40 ms read record from disk
Fourth:	30 ms processing
	140 ms total elapsed time

In the system having no buffering ability the total processing time for four transactions is 140 times 4, or 560 ms, a little more than half a second. On the other hand, the processing time of the partially buffered computer for these same four transactions is 430 ms. The sequence of events is presented schematically in Figure 5.3a. In this system only one channel (path for transferring data between auxiliary storage and main computer memory) is needed to effectively utilize the hardware capabilities of the central processor.

For fully buffered computers, the total elapsed time is 230 ms. and is shown in Figure 5.3b. When comparing the thruput of the four types of computers, shown in Table 5.1, Type 3 computer has the hardware capability of 144 percent greater thruput than Type 1, and 91 percent greater thruput when compared with Type 2b. The overlapping capa-

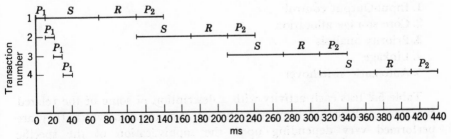

Figure 5.3a P_1, first processing; S, seek; Read, read; P_2, second processing.

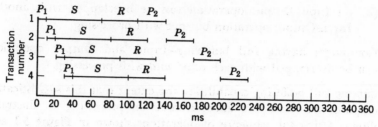

Figure 5.3b Computer with full buffering circuitry (type 3).

bility of a computer directly affects the potential thruput of a computer system.

TABLE 5.1 Comparative Processor Utilization, Percent

CPU Type	Time (ms)	CPU 1 as a Base	CPU 2 as a Base
1	560		
2	430	27.9%	
3	230	144.0%	91.0%

MULTIPROGRAMMING

Multiprogramming is the capability of a computer to overlap the processing of two or more transactions—that is, to have more than one partially processed transaction in the computer at the same time.

The minimum requirements for multiprogramming are a partially buffered computer *and* a group of control routines (often referred to as an operating system, executive control program, or a control program). The operating system should have some, but preferably all, of the following capabilities:

1. Input-Output control
2. Core storage allocation
3. Priority analysis
4. Linkage
5. Automatic switchover

Table 5.2 lists each activity with a description of some of the related functions. These functions as well as the manner in which they are performed vary depending upon the sophistication of the specific operating system. The main technique for increasing thruput in a multiprogramming environment is to use the time when processing cannot continue for one transaction to process another.

TABLE 5.2 System Control Functions

Activity	Functions Performed
1. Input-Output control	a. Send data and control information to (and from) terminals b. Initiate requests, send and receive data from auxiliary storage; disks, tapes, card readers, punches, console typewriters, etc. c. Send and receive data from another computer (core to core transmission)

2. Core storage allocation	a. Provide storage on demand for:
	  1. programs
	  2. data records
	  3. input transactions
	b. Maintain information concerning the status and availability of core storage

3. Priority analysis	Process transactions in a sequence different than the order in which they were received
4. Linkage	a. Accept, as well as transfer, control from one program to another b. Ability to link related transactions, data records and operational programs
5. Automatic switchover	Ability to transfer control upon recognition of equipment malfunction (Applicable only to system having two or more interconnected computers)

Figure 5.4 is a schematic of three transactions, each embodying the processing sequence shown in Figure 5.1. They are being processed in a multiprogrammed operating environment within a buffered computer. Increased thruput is achieved by utilization of time required to obtain a data record from auxiliary storage for the first transaction to process the second. If there is time available during the processing of the second transaction a third will commence processing. It should be noted that:

1. Increased thruput is only possible when there is more than one transaction to be processed.

2. Hardware interrupts trigger the transfers from one transaction to another. The various interrupts are allocated different levels of hardware priority. In most machines it is possible, though in most

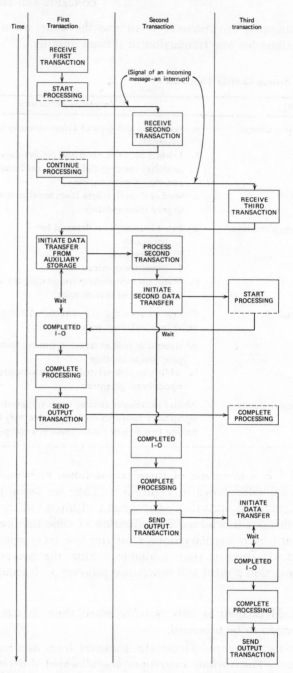

Figure 5.4 Simplified schematic of processing in a multiprogrammed environment.

82

instances not desirable, to prevent interrupts whenever desired. This would be a programmable function.

REENTRANT PROGRAMMING

Many operating systems are so constructed that they permit, if the programmer observes certain rules, more than one transaction by using the same copy of an operational program. The four transactions shown in Figure 5.3, if reentrant, could use the same copy of the operational program, thus reducing the number of program call-ins from auxiliary storage. Some of the rules, which make reentrant programs possible are as follows:

1. All switches, intermediate totals and the like are set in separate blocks of storage rather than within the program. There is one specific block for each transaction, thus ensuring that the program remains unchanged—available for processing other transactions.

2. When an interrupt occurs during the processing of a transaction, the address of the next instruction to be executed, plus registers, are transferred to (saved in) this block of storage. They are restored when control is once again returned to the program for the continuation of processing of a transaction.

3. The operating system is aware of the status of each transaction as well as all data records and location of the next instruction to be executed.

II. SPECIFYING THE CENTRAL PROCESSING UNIT(S)

The steps involved in specifying the type and number of central processing unit (s) needed for the Real-Time system being designed are

    (a) determining the processing required
    (b) deciding on duplexing
    (c) selecting an operating system
    (d) ascertaining core storage and transaction processing time

DETERMINING THE PROCESSING REQUIRED

Converting manual procedures into computerized data processing requires changes to existing processing sequences. This conversion begins with the formulation of functional specifications.

Functional specifications are the first, and highest level of generalization of what eventually becomes input to the next level of detail—that is, program specifications and the block diagramming of operational programs. In the development of generalized functional specifications as with other phases of system design, the direction of activities evolves from the general to the specific. Thus, the *first* draft of functional specifications for operational programs represents *preliminary* thoughts which will be refined and revised until final approval. Before the development of specifications can begin, the analyst must be familiar with

(a) the requirements of management as specified and documented by the steering committee at the inception of the system study, and

(b) existing procedures which were documented for each of the applications.

Functional specifications set forth the work that is to be accomplished. There are two levels of specifications. One is a general description of the processing that is required for the application and would contain the types of transactions that will be accepted, the files that will be updated, and other such tasks. The other level is a detailed description of each input, the files accessed, the processing, and the output transaction(s).

Application Specification—General Description

The following is an example of the functional specifications that were developed for a Sales-Order Application.

January 22, 19____

_____ CORPORATION

FUNCTIONAL SPECIFICATIONS: SALES-ORDER ENTRY

1. *General Description of the Processing of the System*

   The Real-Time system will generate documents required to fill the customer's orders within the time period specified by management. The receipt of an order from any of the retail stores will automatically check and update the inventory on hand, route the order to the nearest warehouse, automatically

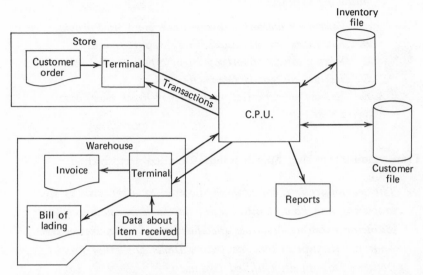

creating the invoice and bill of lading. The customer's account will also be updated automatically with information reflecting the status of his account.

2. Information to be Available from the System:

A. The quantity on hand for any item in any warehouse.
B. The quantities sold per month for the last six months.
C. The number of items returned.
D. The balance owed by the customer.
E. Date of his last order and the amount of his last order.
F. Customer's credit rating.
G. Delivery dates requested by the customer on all unfilled orders.
H. The discounts given to the customer (type and amount).
I. Comparison of the quantity ordered by him this year as against the year before (total and type).
J. Invoices.
K. Bills of Lading.
L. Back-order Notices.
M. Out-of-stock Notices.
N. Receipt of new inventory.

In addition to the generation of invoices and bills of lading, the computer will store information for the output of the following reports:

A. *Customer activity reports—once every two weeks.*
B. *Inventory status and activity report—weekly.*
C. *Sales analysis report by item, type, etc.—monthly.*
D. *Report on goods returned—weekly.*
E. *Report of cancellation of orders—once every two weeks.*

Transaction Processing Specifications—Detailed Descriptions

The second section, for each application, is a synopsis of the processing and flow of information for each transaction. The following example describes specifications for two transactions —one for Receipt of New Inventory Items, the other for Delivery Date of all Unfilled Orders.

January 22, 19_____

_____ CORPORATION

RECEIPT OF NEW INVENTORY: FUNCTIONAL SPECIFICATIONS

Each item received by the warehouse will be entered via a terminal. The inventory number, count, and date will be entered for each item. The information will be checked for correctness, i.e., valid inventory number, valid date, and missing fields. Once checked an acknowledgement of the item received will be sent, by the computer, to the terminal that entered the item. The computer will

(a) update the inventory file.

(b) check to see if the item is in stock. If affirmative the computer will direct a message (invoice and bill of lading) to the warehouse to ship the item(s) to the customer. As a consequence the customer file will be updated.

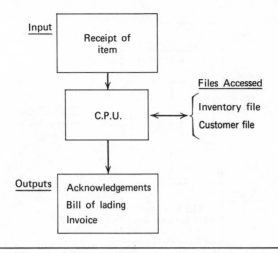

January 22, 19____

_____ CORPORATION

DELIVERY DATE OF ALL UNFILLED ORDERS

FUNCTIONAL SPECIFICATION

The customer number is entered along with the transaction code identifying the request. The customer file is then scanned and a list of all orders—order number, items ordered and date each order is to be shipped, is then returned to the terminal.

*Note: Back ordered items will **not** be listed unless a delivery date has been promised.*

Developing Functional Specifications

The development of functional specifications is a creative process, so the steps enumerated below should be considered a guide—a method of approach:

1. Using the list of transactions that were developed during the development of systems benchmark, group them according to application. For each application the analyst will review the documentation of presently existing procedures. At this point the analyst must decide, based upon his knowledge of the processing capabilities of

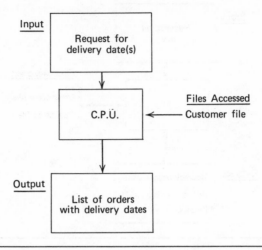

computers, which procedures can be accomplished more efficiently on a computer. These should be listed along with the files required.

2. Review the goals of management as specified by the steering committee and the information obtained from operating management, deciding if any additional processing is to be included. These should be added to the list of computer processing just completed.

3. The list of computer processed information should be documented *in full*. It is reformatted into sentences, for ease of reading, and becomes the first section of the functional specifications of the application. The functional specifications of the Sales-Order Entry Application, shown before, is a list of points which have been assembled into sentences. The addition of a schematic of the flow is useful as an aid to visualization.

4. Using the functional specifications of the application as a guide, the detailed system processing for each transaction can now. be developed. As indicated in the example, they contain more detail than the application specifications. To facilitate preparation of these specifications, the transactions for each application should be separated into inputs and outputs. The analyst should examine each input transaction and ascertain the outputs (transactions) issued by the computer as a result of the receipt of the related input(s). It should be noted that there will be some types of

messages with no inputs; for example, broadcast messages announcing the start of the real-time day.

5. Once all outputs are linked to input transactions, the analyst must ascertain what processing and files are required in order to produce the output transaction. This information, along with the list of outputs and files required, becomes the detailed description of the processing of the functional specifications of the application. Here also the schematic is used for the purpose of visualization.

The documentation of the specifications for *all* of the transactions serves the following purposes:

1. It becomes the input for the specification of the central processing unit(s).
2. It enforces a conclusion as to how the computer will process each transaction.
3. It serves as a guide for detail system specifications (operational program logic) file organization as well as terminal and line requirements.
4. It is a document that can be presented to the steering committee and operating departmental management for approval. Their approval represents agreement that the system as designed at this stage will satisfy the needs and demands of the company.
5. It can be used as a guide, for the training of new members of the real-time system design and implementation team.

DECIDING ON DUPLEXING

Prior to the specification of any equipment, the system analyst must have estimates for the following:

1. the mean time to failure—that is, the estimated number of hours (on the average) that each unit will run before an equipment malfunction occurs.
2. the duration of time (on the average) that it will take to locate the malfunction and repair a unit (called mean time to repair).
3. which unit has the lowest mean time to failure (will break down most often).
4. the cost of duplexing (using a duplicate unit whose purpose is to replace a malfunctioned unit so that the system can continue processing information).

Using this information, the study-team manager can make an initial decision as to whether the company can tolerate these periods of system-component nonavailability. If the data processing requirements are such that the frequency and/or duration of system nonavailability is not tolerable, then some, or all of the units must be duplexed. The decision to duplex can subsequently be modified based upon the development of alternate and less costly techniques for coping with system malfunctions. This decision regarding duplexing should be made *prior* to the specification of each of the components of the system (central processor, auxiliary storage unit, etc.).

SELECTING THE OPERATING SYSTEM

The next step is to select the operating system that is to be used by the real-time system. The specification of the operating system will enable the analyst to determine the amount of core storage and processing time required for control functions, performed by the operating system, as well as the time needed for the processing of transactions.

Specification of the operating system best suited to the needs of the real-time system requires that the system analyst determine which operating system can process the number of transactions, that will be occurring during peak periods, at the most reasonable cost.

The functions performed by the "basic" operating system are complex and involved. Those of an operating system working in a multiprogrammed and/or a multiprocessing real-time environment are understandably much more complicated and involved. If the analyst had *only* to select the operating system which processed the greatest number of transactions, his analysis would require that he select the most sophisticated operating system available. This operating system however would require a large amount of core storage. This can cause an increase in equipment (CPU) costs because when the core storage requirements are expanded, a more expensive processor may be required. There is also a possibility that the more sophisticated operating systems will be able to process many more transactions than are needed to meet system performance requirements. The analyst must, therefore, know how the less sophisticated operating systems function and be ready to translate their operating characteristics into inputs to a simulation model of the system.[3]

Variations as to the extent of multiprogramming permitted will cause changes in the level of thruput that can be maintained. There are various ways control functions are executed by operating systems. Several of these are described in Table 5.3. Alongside each, listed under comments, are the effects the particular technique can have on the design of the system.

It should be noted that no attempt has been made to include all the details of the way in which control functions are implemented. This information is provided in detailed manuals provided by computer manufacturers. The objective of this section is to provide an awareness of the features and limitations of various control techniques so that a review of the detailed functions of any operating system will be more meaningful.

The technique used to maintain "awareness" of the status of all I-Q, the availability of core input transactions awaiting processing and output transactions, is either: (a) to transfer items of work to be done from one list to another, each list containing items all of the same status, or, (b) by changing the status of a transaction within a list, thus scanning will involve working with a list containing dissimilar situations.

Real-Time Intermixed with Batch Processing

A computing system that permits more than one partially processed real-time transaction within the central processor and only *one* batch type application program permitted performs the same functions as in 1.b of the previous table with one exception. That is, whenever there is either transactions in the CPU awaiting the completion of I-O operation, or there are no real-time messages in main computer storage, control is transferred *not* to a waiting loop but to an operational program for the processing of batch-type transactions. Thus during those periods of the day in which there are no, or a minimal number of, real-time transactions, the computer can be utilized more productively.

[3] In the author's opinion accurately determining thruput as well as response time once all equipment has been first specified, in a system utilizing a fully buffered computer, is the main reason for simulation. Many variations to the basic design should be analyzed. Data concerning several types of control programs should be available for input to simulation. If the reader is fortunate and is involved with a system in which there is no doubt that the most sophisticated operating system will be used, simulation will be only of general interest

TABLE 5.3 Only Real-Time Processing [4]

a. One transaction processed at a time—more than one message can be queued within the CPU

Situation Within the Computer	Possible Actions Permitted by the Operating System	Comments
Transaction being processed	Transaction permitted entry into the computer only if sufficient core available.	a. The specification of the amount of storage allocated for input and output messages directly affects the number of transactions that the computer will be able to store (queue internally) b. Transfer of data to or from disk or tape can be overlapped only with the processing requiring the information c. Minimal utilization of available time during disk seeks as only one transaction can be processed at a time.
Processing just completed for a transaction	1. No other transactions waiting for processing in the input area	Control program goes into a "waiting loop." This is standard for dedicated real-time systems. Depending upon the distribution of transaction volumes during non-peak periods, a large percentage of computer processing time can be spent wating for transactions from terminals.[5] One technique to reduce wait time is to confine the span of time allocated for real-time processing, thus having the operating personnel increase the efficiency of the computer system rather than vice-versa.
	2. Other transactions in the input area waiting to be processed	The next transaction is selected. The selection can be made on the basis of first in, first processed or by the recognition of one or more different priorities. The number of levels of priorities of input transactions varies depending upon the computer(s) and the operating system. Within any one priority, transactions are processed in the order they enter the main computer.

[4] This is called a dedicated system. During the hours allocated for real-time processing, no batch-type data processing is permitted.

[5] Most computers permit interrupts from outside of the main processor-request from terminals, completion of transmissions, or completion of seeks. There are computers which allow masking (no interrupts allowed) of these interrupts under special situations.

b. The operating system can support more than one partially processed transaction with the central processor.

Situation Within the Computer	Possible Actions Permitted by the Operating System	Comments
Transaction being processed— a terminal requesting to send a message to the computer	1. Transaction not permitted entry if no available core. 2. Transaction always permitted entry. If not enough core will be queued on disk.	When the transaction being processed must temporarily halt as: (a) a real-time operational processing program must be read into core, or (b) a data record is required; control is transferred to a section of the operating system which determines what other processing is possible, and can result in: (1) doing nothing else, i.e., all transactions are awaiting the completion of an I-O Operation. Operating system goes into a "waiting loop" or a "wait state" awaiting an interrupt, (2) there is at least one other transaction that has its I-O record(s) and processing program ready. Control is transferred (or returned to) that operational program and processing continues. The convention most often used is that control is given to the program whose transaction can now continue being processed and who came into core storage first (assuming no overriding priority of processing; i.e., higher on list of transactions that can be processed). This checking of the list takes place only when an interrupt of any type has taken place.
Processing completed for a transaction	The transaction is eliminated from all lists. The core held for that transaction is released and now available for a new transaction; its program and data records. Control is transferred to: (a) a "waiting loop"—if no other processing can take place or (b) to the operational program that can begin, or continue processing the next transaction on the list.	

A minor variation to this limitation of one batch type application program is that some operating systems will permit an additional I-O to I-O transfer program, (disk to printer, copy disk, card to disk, etc.). This is considered to be a limited extension to the operating system—assuming a low priority of processing time.

A more sophisticated version of the above system is one that allows more than one partially processed real-time transaction within the central processor and *more than one* batch-type application program permitted—that is, a program for payroll calculation and an inventory control program might be in core storage at the same time; each capable of having a partially processed transaction.

In the operating system described above, whenever the *batch program* has a tape or disk I-O operation the computer goes into a "waiting loop" until an interrupt takes place. In an operating system permitting more than one "batch type program" control is transferred to the highest lower priority batch program that is capable of processing. If all of the batch programs have transactions awaiting the completion of an I-O operation the operating system goes into a wait state.

At this level of sophistication, the systems analyst, rather than the operating system, specifies the maximum number of real-time transactions. This is done when specifying real-time/batch program core requirements. The number of subroutines that will be core resident for this one application batch program is a function of the amount of core storage allocated to the application program. Small amounts of core storage allocated to the batch type program can require program overlaps.

Operating systems with their many levels of sophistication have been developed to improve the productive utilization of the computer. It might appear that the most sophisticated operating system should always be the one to use. There are certain guidelines, however, that must be kept in mind by the analyst when he is determining which operating system to use:

1. The more sophisticated the operating system the more core storage required.
2. The more sophisticated the operating system the more time required within it to execute its many functions.
3. To support the more sophisticated operating system additional I-O devices may be required.
4. The utilization of the system may be so high that little additional benefit can be obtained by specification of a more sophisticated operating system.

5. The more multiprogramming taking place the greater the possibility for problems to arise during implementation of the system.

Selecting an operating system first involves using the *projected* peak period transaction volumes, developed when determining systems performance requirements, to eliminate those operating systems which appear to be unable to process the expected transaction volume. If more than one operating system can process the expected number of transactions a relative weighting of each using the following factors, should be made:

1. The amount of core storage required.
2. The time that the computer spends "in the supervisor"—that is, the percentage of available time the computer spends executing instructions that are a part of the operating system (called *overhead*).
3. The extent that the computer overlaps functions.
4. The degree of upward compatability with more powerful operating systems.
5. The various "miscellaneous" features which, as a part of the operating system, reduce the amount of programming and/or the time required learning to use the system.
6. Extent of programmer involvement—that is, the constraints and complexity of the operating system as related to the time needed to learn the operating system.

There can be no fast rules for the specification of an operating system as the factors affecting the decision vary. The lack of programming personnel may be a major consideration in one instance while a core storage constraint may be of primary concern in another. Each of these constraints could justify the selection of a different operating system. In the final analysis, the *critical factor* is the ability of operating systems to maintain the required level of transaction processing (thruput).

With the specification of an operating system, the analyst can then obtain the following information from the computer manufacturer:

1. The execution time of the various functions of the operating system.
2. The core storage required for those functions necessary for the processing of real-time transactions.

The next step is to determine the storage and the execution time requirements of the real-time operation programs. This information will be needed to determine if the central processor(s) being analyzed can maintain the required thruput during peak periods.

ASCERTAINING CORE STORAGE AND TRANSACTION PROCESSING TIME

Determining storage requirements and processing time involves analysis of transaction processing logic. There are various ways of documenting this processing logic. They are shown in Table 5.4. Alongside each are the advantages or disadvantages.

TABLE 5.4 Formats for Documentation of Operational Program Specifications

Type	Advantages	Disadvantages	
Written descriptions	Easy to complete	Difficult to use when determining program execution time	
Detailed flow charts	Can be given to the programmer for coding	Too much detail for this stage	Major revisions to the document required when changes to specifications take place
Decision tables	Complete logic documentation	Same as above	Same as above
Summarized block diagrams	High level but containing minimum of detail. Easy to make revisions		

For the reasons stated in the table, Summarized block diagrams are best suited for determining core storage and timing estimates. Analyzing block diagrams is the simplest way of

(a) estimating operation program execution time,
(b) determining within each program the points at which file records (storage on auxiliary storage) are required,
(c) estimating main memory storage requirements, and
(d) supplying the information to be used to develop detailed flow diagrams and decision tables for the programs to be written during implementation of the system.

Summarized block diagrams are high-level flow diagrams structured in a manner that separates

(a) the internal processing logic from Input-Output functions,
(b) all major decision breaks.

Accompanying each decision break should be an estimate of that percentage of the total number of transactions that will be leaving the decision break. An example of two summarized block diagrams, developed for a sales order application, are shown in Figures 5.5 and 5.6. In Figure 5.5, the decision break labeled "Customer Order Contains Back Ordered Item" 90 percent do not contain a back ordered item while 10 percent do. The significance of the 10 percent is that, on the average, one out of every ten transactions will require an additional record from auxiliary storage, a significant increase in total processing time. Included for each customer order containing a back order is the distribution of back orders—that is, the percentage of these orders having 1, 2, 3, etc. items that require back ordering. The next step, estimating the processing time required for each phase (box on the summarized block diagram), have been included with the diagram shown in Figure 5.6.

When preparing summarized block diagrams the following rules should be adhered to:

1. Inputs and outputs from secondary storage, as well as to and from the terminals, are separated from main computer processing.
2. Any block of operational program execution must not include any "major" decision breaks. Major decisions are those types for which there is a substantial difference in processing time if one path is taken rather than the other. To combine both paths into one block would give a distorted picture of the processing time required for the transaction. As shown in Figures 5.5 and 5.6, the percentages of transactions that take one path rather than the other has been included. By structuring the operational program specifications in this manner the analyst is able to channel these diagrams directly to those concerned with File Organization, Control Program Specification, and determining total systems processing time (either by simulation or analytical techniques).

Using the list of transactions developed in the analysis of system requirements, the analyst must develop summarized block diagrams for *each* transaction that will take place during the real-time day. He does this first listing the functions to be performed, including the information that must be obtained from disk storage in order to process the transaction. The following list of functions is required for recording the customer order shown in Figure 5.6:

1. Determine if all fields of the input message are valid.
2. Obtain the customer record.

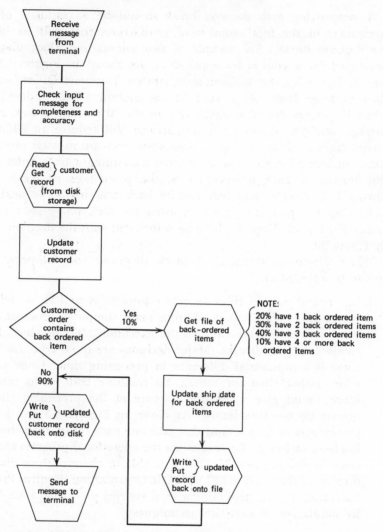

Figure 5.5. Change shipping date on a customer's order.

3. If this is a credit sale save amount of credit and check to see if he is allowed credit.

4. Obtain inventory record.

5. If sufficient quantity reduce balance on hand.

6. Determine price (quantity x unit price less discount).

7. Repeat steps 5, 6, and 7 until all items ordered have been processed.

Note: 60 percent of all orders have 3 to 5 items. (Note: if any

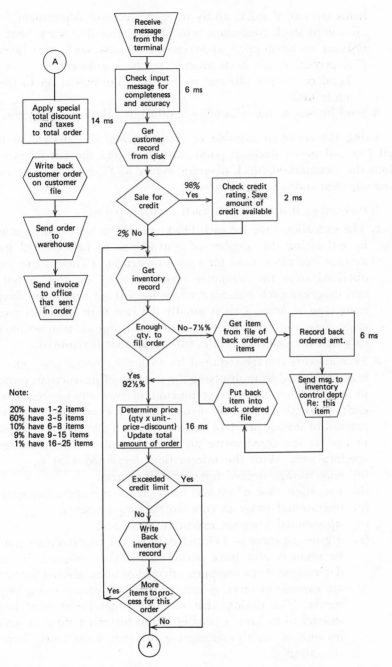

Figure 5.6 Recording customer's order.

The flowchart contains the following elements:

Receive message from the terminal

Check input message for completeness and accuracy — 6 ms

Get customer record from disk

Sale for credit — 98% Yes → Check credit rating. Save amount of credit available — 2 ms

2% No

Get inventory record

Enough qty. to fill order — No-7½% → Get item from file of back ordered items → Record back ordered amt. — 6 ms → Send msg. to inventory control dept Re: this item → Put back item into back ordered file

Yes 92½%

Determine price (qty x unit-price-discount) Update total amount of order — 16 ms

Exceeded credit limit — Yes

No

Write Back inventory record

More items to process for this order — Yes / No

A

A (top left)

Apply special total discount and taxes to total order — 14 ms

Write back customer order on customer file

Send order to warehouse

Send invoice to office that sent in order

Note:

20% have 1-2 items
60% have 3-5 items
10% have 6-8 items
9% have 9-15 items
1% have 16-25 items

items are out of stock, notify inventory control department). Store all out of stock conditions into file of items that have been back ordered to be shipped upon receipt of new stock into inventory (7½ percent of all items ordered are back ordered).

Total customer's bill and record this information on to the customer file.

8. Send invoice to the sales office and bill of lading to warehouse.

Using the above as a guide to diagramming, the analyst identified all I-O and major decision points and organized the list of functions into the summarized block diagram shown in Figure 5.6. The following was then added to the diagram:

1. Percentage distribution at each decision point.

2. The execution time for each block—execution time was determined by estimating the number of instructions to be executed by the average execution time for each instruction. (These items can be obtained from the computer manufacturer.) As the analyst lists and diagrams each transaction type he will see that many have the same type of flow. This is usually the case with inquiries. At this stage these can be grouped together. Listing all transaction types to which the diagram applies will be all that is required.

3. Estimate core storage required for each operational program. This is accomplished by multiplying the number of instructions estimated in step 2 times the average amount of core storage required for each instruction. To this figure should be added an additional amount of storage; a safety factor (of at least 20 percent is advisable) in case of too conservative an estimate and/or minor changes in specifications. With the information developed—that is,

   (a) core storage needed for operating system,
   (b) execution time of various functions of the operating system,
   (c) operational program core storage requirements,
   (d) operational program execution time, and
   (e) a gross estimate of I-O and data record requirements (later to be refined) plus peak period transaction volumes, it can be determined if the computers that have been selected for analysis are capable of meeting system performance processing requirements. The timings that have been developed must be considered to be gross estimates as the increased thruput, possible because of multiprogramming, has not been taken into consideration.

If the computer(s) being studied is capable of meeting system performance requirements then this phase of the study is completed. If the computer selected is found wanting then reanalysis is required. A more powerful operating system, a faster computer, or more storage must be considered. The analyst will have to recycle through many of the steps discussed in this chapter until a *satisfactory* computer has been selected.

CONCLUSION

Specifying the central processing unit(s) required involves the following:

1. Formulation of general functional specifications.
2. Development of detailed descriptions of inputs, processing, and output transactions.
3. Determining the extent to which there will be duplexing of equipment.
4. Selection of an operating system.
5. Estimation of core storage requirements.
6. Determination of program execution time—I-O timing estimates.
7. Selecting a computer(s) which can meet system performance processing requirements.

CHAPTER 6

File Requirements of the System

PROCESSING MESSAGES IN A REAL-TIME ENVIRONMENT REQUIRES THAT THE COMPUTER BE ABLE TO RETRIEVE AND UPDATE MANY TYPES OF DATA ON AN IMMEDIATE RESPONSE BASIS. IT IS NEITHER TECHNICALLY NOR ECONOMICALLY FEASIBLE TO STORE WITHIN THE MAIN COMPUTER ALL THE DATA AND PROGRAMS NECESSARY FOR REAL-TIME PROCESSING OF TRANSACTIONS. IT IS THE JOB OF THE SYSTEMS ANALYST TO FIND THE CHEAPEST STORAGE DEVICE(S) NEEDED TO MAINTAIN THE REQUIRED THRUPUT. IN THIS CHAPTER, SECTION I, CONCEPTS AND TERMS, DEFINES WHAT THE SYSTEMS ANALYST MUST KNOW BEFORE HE IS ABLE TO DETERMINE THE FILE REQUIREMENTS. SECTION II ANALYZES HOW TO DETERMINE THE FILE REQUIREMENTS OF A REAL-TIME SYSTEM.

I. CONCEPTS AND TERMS

When selecting the auxiliary storage devices needed for the system being designed, the systems analyst must first determine those units which are compatible with the computer that has been selected. For each type of auxiliary storage device selected, the analyst must learn their capacity and how they store and retrieve data. This information is then used to determine the following:

1. the amount of space (in each unit) available for the storing of data.
2. the time required to find and retrieve a required record, and
3. the time needed to transfer the record, once it is found
   (a) from the device to main computer memory as well as,
   (b) from the computer to the device, after the record has been processed and/or created.

The types of units available for storing information in machine intelligible form can be categorized as *random access* and *sequential devices.*

RANDOM ACCESS STORAGE DEVICES

Physical attributes

There are three major types of random access storage units: Disks, Drums, and Cartridge type devices.

Disks

Though the capacity and time required to retrieve records may differ, disks are constructed in a similar manner. Disk units are continuous motion devices, as opposed to cartridge type devices which are start (and) stop type units, and consist of two major components: read-write access mechanisms and disk surfaces.

Read-Write Access Mechanisms. These mechanisms, consist of a read-write head (point *A* in Figure 6.1a), an access arm (*B* in Figure 6.1a), and an access assembly (*C* in the figure). Their purpose is to provide a path for data coming from the computer, via the disk control unit, to the disk surface, and vice versa. Depending upon the model, arm movement can be one of three types. If there is only one access mechanism attached to an access assembly (and more than one disk surface) arm action is horizontal as well as vertical. To move the access arm from point *A* to point *B*, shown in Figure 6.1b, requires: (a) horizontal movement (to move the arm clear of the disk surface), (b) vertical movement, to move the *same* arm to the new disk surface, and (c) horizontal movement to move the arm to the track specified in the seek command. Another type is a disk storage unit having multiple arm mechanisms attached to one access assembly (see Figure 6.1c).

There is one read-write mechanism (head) for each surface. The arms are so constructed that all read-write mechanisms are aligned vertically, one under the other. To move one arm requires the movement of all the arms. On the completion of an I-O operation that involved moving the access mechanism that was located on track *A* (of Figure 6.1c) to data located on track *B*, requires only horizontal arm movement. If, on completion of the transfer of data that involved track *A*, data are to be read next from track *C*, *no* arm movement is required because of the vertical alignment to the read-write heads. Only head-switching is needed. Head-switching, the changing of the specified read-write mechanism by computer command, is performed electronically. This vertical alignment of read-write heads and disk tracks has given rise to the *cylinder concept.* A cylinder is composed of all the vertically aligned tracks for which a multiple arm access mechanism, when positioned over one track, is able to access without an additional arm movement. Cylinders, a conceptual way of viewing disk tracks, are important when determining record access times since they represent the maximum number of characters that can be accessed with one seek instruction. For instance, a disk unit having 150 tracks on each surface with a total of 10 disk surfaces on the drive is considered to have 150 cylinders, each cylinder containing 10 tracks. Figure 6.2 is a drawing of an IBM 2311. In this schematic there are 203 tracks per disk surface and ten disk

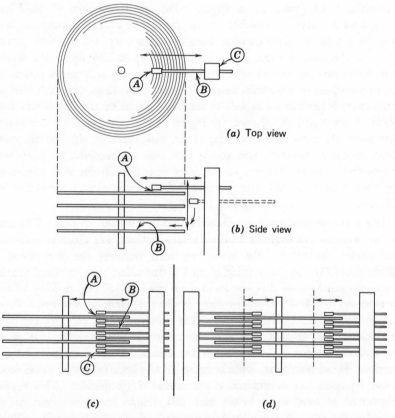

Figure 6.1. Representative disk mechanism (schematic). Some manufacturers produce disk drives with the disk surfaces mounted vertically.

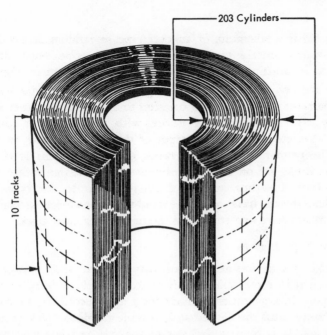

Figure 6.2. Schematic of disk cylinder. Reprinted by permission from IBM, "Introduction to IBM System/360 Direct Access Storage Devices and Organization Methods," Manual No. C20–1649, p. 11, © by International Business Machines Corporation.

surfaces. The unit can therefore be considered to have a total of 203 cylinders.

Disk Surfaces. Though the size and usage differ, the storing of data on a disk is similar to recording on a phonograph record. Whereas music is recorded on one continuous track that ends near the center of the record, a disk surface used for storing data consists of concentric circles or tracks. (It should be noted that some disk devices sub-divide a track into sections—called sectors. With these disk devices one sector represents the *minimum* amount of data that can be transferred). The access arm, unlike the recording and playing arm of a phonograph, does not touch the surface of the disk. Every track in a set of disk surfaces [1] has a pre-assigned number which is used during data transfer operations.

---

[1] Disk surfaces contained in a removable disk are called a disk pack. If the disks cannot be removed they are called a module. As the trend is toward flexibility this term, disk pack, will be used when referring to all tracks and surfaces accessible to a computer from *one* disk drive.

Drums

Figure 6.3 is a schematic of another type of random access device, a drum. Drums contain tracks and an access mechanism(s) similar to those used in multiple arm disk storage devices, shown in Figure 6.1c.

There are two types of drum storage devices: small capacity storage units capable of high speed data transfers to and from computer memory, and large capacity data storage devices with slower transfer rates. The physical characteristics of both types of drums are similar to those of disks. The primary difference between disks and drums is that on a drum the tracks are on the circumference of the device rather than on a flat surface. In other words, a drum is similar to one cylinder of a disk. Some drums have only one read-write head for several tracks, whereas others have one read-write mechanism for each track.

Cartridge Type Devices

Cartridge type devices are high capacity stop-start data storage devices. Data is stored in removable containers (called cells or bins) on strips of mylar tape. Once a request is made for a data record by the computer, the cells move until the desired strip is underneath the pickup head (see Figure 6.4a). It is then pulled out of the cell and wrapped around a drum, shown in Figure 6.4b. Once it is wrapped around the drum the data can be transferred to (or from) computer memory.

Random Access Data Storage Capabilities

Although the entire random access device is physically available for the storage of data, not all of it can be used. Thus, when determining the amount of random access storage for information, one must allow the space required for

(a) record and track identification,
(b) information relating to the length of the data record,
(c) checking the transmission of data, and

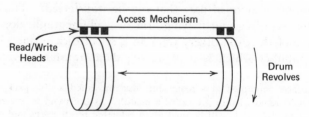

Figure 6.3. A drum storage device (schematic).

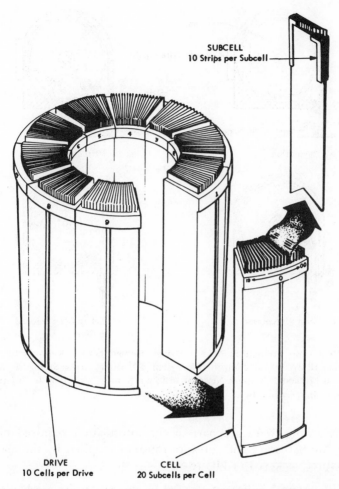

SUBCELL
10 Strips per Subcell

DRIVE
10 Cells per Drive

CELL
20 Subcells per Cell

Figure 6.4a Schematic of a cartridge storage device. Reproduced by permission from IBM, "Introduction to IBM System/360 Direct Access Storage Devices and Organization Methods," Manual No. C20–1649, pp. 8 and 10, © 1966 by International Business Machines Corporation.

(d) the physical requirements of the device.

Figure 6.5 is a schematic of the format of a "standard" track of data. It shows the various types of information, in addition to the actual data, that are required on a track of a random access device. Although the track shown in Figure 6.5 is a particular format used by IBM random access devices, all random access devices require space for the storage of "nondata" information.

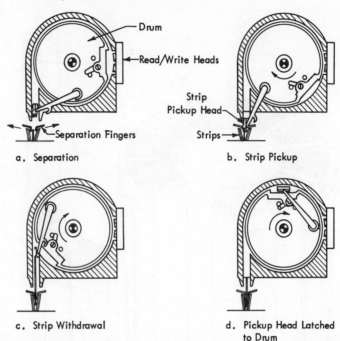

a. Separation   b. Strip Pickup

c. Strip Withdrawal   d. Pickup Head Latched to Drum

Figure 6.4b Pickup mechanism of a cartridge storage device. Reproduced by permission from IBM, "Introduction to IBM System/360 Direct Access Storage Devices and Organization Methods," Manual No. C20–1649, pp. 8 and 10, © 1966 by International Business Machines Corporation.

The following items are part of the information required on each track by the hardware and software routines supplied by the computer manufacturer, as keyed in Figure 6.5:

(a) A physical indication, sensed by the read-write mechanism and circuitry, which indicates the start of the track.

(b) An area, not available for data, called a gap. Although similar to the inter-record gap found on tape, its purpose is to give circuitry within the disk control unit time to compare information just received from the disk surface with the data it has stored. This includes address checking and bit counting.

(c) The home address which contains information indicating the track address.

(d) Record Zero is used to specify an alternate track in the event that the track on which this information should have been placed is defective.

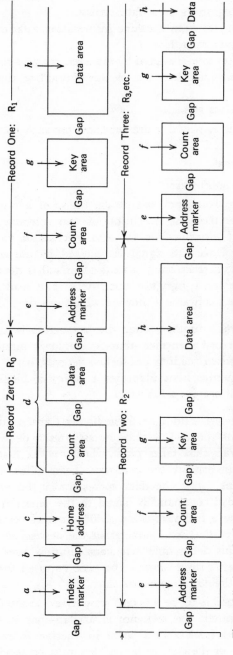

Figure 6.5. A standard track format. Reprinted by permission from IBM, "IBM System/360 Disk Operating System Data Management Concepts," Manual No. C24-3427, p. 40, © 1966 by International Business Machines Corporation.

(e) The address market field is used by the control unit to locate the beginning of a data record.

(f) The count area contains information relating to the length of the data record.

(g) The key area, inserted by the user, contains the record identifier: the part number, the employee number, the account number, etc.

(h) The data record.

Note: (Items *e, f,* and *g* are repeated for each data record.)

Record Retrieval

The Mechanical Process

Transferring data from one of the tracks of a random access device to another, requires the execution of two commands. The first is a seek command which causes the arm mechanism to be moved to the proper track. Once the signal is received by the computer, that the arm is over the correct track, a read command is then given to transfer data from the track into the computer. The read instruction issued by the computer contains a number which can be

(a) the track number, when the instruction is to read a full track,

(b) the record identifier—that is, employee number, part number, etc., when reading unblocked records, or

(c) the number that identifies a group of blocked records which do not occupy a full track.

The data record cannot be immediately transferred since the continuous motion of the disk surface necessitates a delay. This *rotational delay* is the wait that takes place whenever the first character of the record is not underneath the read-write head. This time can vary from practically 0 ms. when the data comes under the read-write head the moment the read command is issued to the time required for the disk surface to come a full revolution (360°) around because the read-write head just missed the first character of the desired record. The analyst, when taking this delay time into consideration, uses $\frac{1}{2}$ the maximum (360°) delay as his time factor. The time required for a disk to revolve 180° is called the "average access time."

When a record is to be written, transferred to auxiliary storage from the main computer, the sequence is similar—that is, the arm is moved to the required track and a write instruction is executed. The core storage address of the data to be written must be specified to trigger the transfer. On completion of the recording of the data onto auxiliary storage, a "write check" may be executed. A write check is a comparison of the data which has just been recorded with either the data in core storage or a regeneration of the count of bits generated when the data was recorded. An unequal comparison (or count) will result in an error condition signal being sent to the computer.

Record Retrieval Techniques

Since a random access device is one in which it is not necessary to read all the data records that are physically stored between the beginning of the device and the location of the desired record, the steps for obtaining a record [2] are: first determine the track on which the record is stored (located), move the access arm to that track and then transfer the record from the device into computer memory. There are three ways that data stored on random access devices can be retrieved—Directly, Sequentially with Indexes, and Sequentially.

Direct Retrieval of Stored Data. This technique uses a formula to convert the record identification (number or name) into one of the pre-numbered track addresses. For example, if a file consists of 2,500 major subassembly part numbers, by using the size of each record, an initial estimate can be made of the number of part records that can be stored on each track. The total number of tracks required for storing the file can then be determined. Assume for purposes of this example, that 600 tracks of auxiliary storage were allocated to store a parts file— track numbered 0101 of 0700. The part numbers are 6 digits and range between 208701 and 946818.

One tested formula for randomizing is to multiply the part number by the number of tracks allocated to the file, 600. The three high order digits of the product are then added to the starting track address. For part number 461290, the track address is 377:

$$461290 \times 600 = 276774000$$
$$276 + 101 = 377$$

This technique should be tested with all the part numbers to determine the number of overflow records that are generated. Overflow records are those which must be stored in a location other than the track address generated by the randomizing formula. They occur when the formula

---

[2] Unless the arm is held (no arm movement is permitted after reading data into computer memory until the record is written back onto an existing file) writing a record involves the steps discussed previously. In a pure sequential environment, a seperate section of auxiliary storage is required for writing records.

creates the same track address for more records than there is space available on that track.

Overflow records are not desirable because they increase the time required to locate those types of records—that is, if a generated address does not contain the record, the overflow location, specified on the generated track, must then be read. Thus an extra read and rotational delay take place before the overflow record can be available for processing.

Another randomizing technique is prime number division. The closest prime number to 600 (the total number of available tracks) 599, is used. Part numbers are divided by 599, and the remainder constitutes the number which when added to the starting track address determines the track address at which each data record is to be stored: $461290 \div 599 = 770$ with a remainder of 60. The record for part number 461290 using prime number division would be stored in location 161 (60 + 101). The total number of overflow records developed with this technique should be ascertained and compared to the number developed using the first formula. If this data file were to be stored randomly, the technique which developed the fewer number of overflow records is the one that would be selected.[3]

The following are of concern when storing records "randomly":

1. Provided there is not an excessive number of overflow records in an I-O bound system, records can be retrieved more quickly using this technique.
2. Whenever there is a small percentage of input transactions, presorting the transactions so they can be run against the file sequentially is of minimum value.
3. The more even the distribution of record identification numbers the less the number of overflows.
4. The formula that is developed may not be satisfactory in the future due to changes in the distribution of record identification numbers caused by additions and deletions of part numbers.
5. To develop a good randomizing formula requires time. There is no guarantee that a formula can be developed that is better (faster record accessing) than the utilization of some other organization technique.
6. Random loading of data gives a lower percentage of packing (percentage of available space that is used for storing data). Eighty per-

[3] For additional randomizing techniques as well as an interesting analysis of file organization which includes a bibliography of articles on the subject, see "File Organization and Addressing," Buchholz, Werner, IBM Systems Journal, Vol. 2, June, 1963, pp. 86-111.

cent utilization for random files is considered good. 95 percent utilization is possible for a sequentially organized file. Lower percentages of packing require more storage space.

Sequential Storage/Retrieval of Data with Indexes. With this technique, data records are stored in sequence, usually ascending. Indexes are also created when the data records are loaded onto the storage device. These indexes facilitate the location and transfer of a desired record without having to read every record stored on the preceding tracks. By using the same part numbers exemplified for loading randomly, 208701 through 946818, it was estimated that six records could be stored on a track. (Formulas are available to ascertain track capacities.) Thus the assignment of auxiliary storage for the first 30 records with the tracks they would be stored on (starting in this example with track 104) are shown in Table 6.1.

TABLE 6.1

Part Number	Track Assigned	Part Number	Track Assigned	Part Number	Track Assigned
208943	104	216144	105	222171	107
212144	104	216521	105	222173	107
212691	104			222421	107
214004	104	216817	106	222681	107
215103	104	220048	106		
215432	104	220049	106	222739	108
		220384	106	222896	108
215482	105	220588	106	224372	108
215483	105	221114	106	224410	108
215619	105			224981	108
216101	105	222169	107	224988	108
		222170	107		

The first level index (pointer) to be developed by the loading program specifies the highest part number stored on each track.

LEVEL 1 INDEXES

104	215432
105	216521
106	221114
107	222681
108	224988
:	:
417	946818

The Level 1 indexes should be stored in a location that would minimize seek time. The 2,500 part numbers will require 417 tracks (2500 records ÷ 6 records to the track + enough tracks to store 417 first level index entries. Since each index entry requires 9 characters, two or three tracks, depending upon the device, would be required for the storage of index entries for Level 1 indexes. The first level indexes could be stored on tracks 101, 102, and 103. Storing of indexes must be planned for when determining auxiliary storage requirements. In files with large numbers of Level 1 indexes a second level of indexes could be created to eliminate the need for scanning all of the Level 1 indexes. It is the Level 1 indexes that are used to build second level indexes. In our example only 3 second level indexes would be created. Each second level index entry would represent the highest part number referenced on *each* level 1 index track.

101	488692 (the highest part number stored on index track 101 is 488692)
102	794088 (the highest part number stored on index track 102 is 794088)
103	946818 (the highest part number stored on index track 103 is 946818)

In this example, since there are only three entries on the second level index (27 character positions), they could be stored as a table in a core storage. When working with files with a large number of records, a second level of indexes can require several thousand character positions of storage. In this situation the secondary level could be stored on secondary storage with possibly third level indexes created and stored in computer memory. The purpose of creating these various levels of indexes is to reduce the time required to find the level 1 index that specifies the track location of the desired record. Indexes are accessed as follows: a transaction enters the system updating the quantity field of part number 220588, and a *compare* is made with the first entry in the highest level index in this case the second level index. Since 488692 is higher than part number 220588, the indexes on track 101 are read into core storage (that is, the next level index is on track 101). (A high compare indication, a compare with a Branch or High instruction being executed, means that we have the desired entry). A similar comparison with the Level 1 index shows that the part number we are looking for, 220588, is not stored on track 104 because the Level 1 index entry 215432 is lower than the desired part number. If the record is not stored on track number 104, another compare with the next Level 1 is made. The highest part number stored on track 105 is part number 216521, which is also lower. The next compare shows that the part number on the index is higher than the part number of the input transaction. This is the lowest level index which this means that the record is stored on track number 106 and can now be transferred from track 106 into core storage for processing.

Storing data sequentially with indexes offers the following advantages:

1. A high percentage of packing is possible.

2. It takes advantage of the random accessing ability of the device while storing the data sequentially.

3. It is comparatively easy to create. Standard computer manufacturer utility routines can be used if desired to load the file.

4. The distribution of record numbers can be clustered.

5. Additions can easily be included in the file. If there is room on a track a record can be added. If there is no room on the track the record is stored on an overflow track with the track address of the record being stored on the track in special link field. Link fields must be made a part of every record on the file by the file loading program. Link fields remain zeros until a record has been loaded in the overflow area.

Sequential Retrieval of Data. Storing data on a random access file in this manner utilizes the same techniques as data stored on tape. Since there is no way of going directly to the record (no randomizing or indexing techniques accompany sequentially stored data), processing a file thus requires the consecutive reading of all of the files (tracks containing information). Tables, working areas, programs, or any type of information required in its entirety is suited for sequential storage. With random access storage it is possible to divide the storage unit (the pack) into sections while maintaining a directory of the location of each section. It is then possible, by searching the directory, to go directly to the desired section of random access storage.

TRANSFER RATES

Regardless of the type of device the rate in which data can be transferred is a factor that concerns the system analyst. Transfer rates can vary from 15,000 to 300,000 characters per second. Briefly summarized in Table 6.2 are the approximate speeds, capacities, and transfer rates of the three types of random access devices.

TABLE 6.2

Type Device	Capacity (in millions of characters)	Access Time (ms) Range	Average	Transfer Rate
Disks	2 to 100	25-180	135-165	50 KC to 100 KB*
Drums (high speed)	1.1 to 5	0-17.5	4-8.75	200 KC to 1200 KB 40-55 KB
Cartridges	5 to 400	95 to 600	350-550	

* KC is an abbreviation of thousand characters per second while KB is thousand bytes per second.

Random access storage is an integral part of a real-time system, as it is the only type of auxiliary storage device for which there can be a basically constant time of record retrieval.

SEQUENTIAL STORAGE DEVICES

Physical Characteristics

Sequential access storage devices are those whose data can only be retrieved in the same sequence it was recorded—that is, a specific record can be transferred only after all records preceding it, starting with the first, have been read. Cards and tapes [4] are the two major types of machine intelligible sequential storage. Punched cards because of their limited capacity (a maximum of 80 to 96 characters of information per card), and comparatively slow access (card read/punch) time have minimal applicability in a real-time operating environment. Tapes, because of their capacity, provide large amounts of automatically accessible storage.

A tape drive is a start-stop device. Before a data transfer begins the tape is not in motion. A tape transfer command (a read or write command) causes the tape drive to begin moving the tape. A data transfer does not begin *until* the tape drive begins moving the tape at a prespecified speed. The data transfer then takes place. Upon completion of the data transmission the tape unit begins slowing down the movement of tape across the read-write mechanism (head) of the drive until the physical movement of the tape stops. Execution of the next tape command again causes the tape drive to start moving the tape.

[4] There have been tape drives which are capable of skipping past a prespecified number of records (skipping under segment mark count). This feature improves but does not modify the sequential aspects of tape units.

The section of tape that is moved during the time the drive is building up speed as well as when it is coming to a halt is called an interrecord gap, and is unusable for the storage of data. Figure 6.6 is a schematic of an interrecord gap.

Data Storage Capabilities

The capacity of a tape is dependent upon five factors, each of which can considerably effect the amount of information that can be stored on one reel. These variables are the

(a) physical length of the tape,
(b) density of the data,
(c) size of the interrecord gap,
(d) blocking factor, and
(e) packing ability of the tape unit

The physical length of the tape

Tapes are obtainable in lengths up to 2400 feet. The longer the length of the tape on the reel the greater the amount of data that can be stored.

Density of the data

Density is the number of data characters that it is possible to store on one inch of tape. All other things being equal the higher the density the greater the amount of information stored on a reel. Tape densities are expressed as cpi (characters per inch) or bpi (bits per inch). Informa-

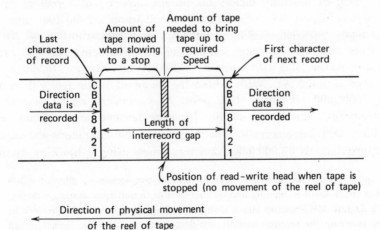

Figure 6.6. An interrecord gap.

tion recorded on a tape at 800 cpi means that 800 characters (if there is no intervening interrecord gap) can be stored on one inch of tape.

The size of the interrecord gap

As mentioned previously, the interrecord gap represents wasted space —space unavailable for the storage of data. The capacity of a reel of tape is thus directly related to the size and number of interrecord gaps located throughout the reel. The size of the interrecord gap is a function of the braking and starting ability of the tape unit. Representative sizes of interrecord gaps are $3/4$ of an inch, $6/10$ of an inch, $45/100$ of an inch and $38/100$ of an inch. The number of interrecord gaps interspersed throughout a tape file (of information) is a function of the blocking factor.

Blocking Factor

The blocking factor specifies the number of logical records contained in a physical record.[5] A physical record is the total number of characters physically transferred into core storage on a read command, or written upon execution of a write instruction. A logical record is all the information related to *one* transaction or master record. A blocking factor of 5 thus means that every time a physical record is transferred it contains 5 logical records. In this instance there will be only one interrecord gap between each of 5 records. A blocking factor of 1 indicates that a physical record consists of only 1 logical record. There will therefore be an interrecord gap between each record on the file. The effect of blocking factors on storage capacity of a reel of tape is charted in Figure 6.7. This chart is based upon a 2400 foot tape with data being recorded at 800 cpi with $6/10$ inch interrecord gaps. In this example one reel of tape containing 100 character records with a blocking factor of 5 will contain 11,500,000 characters (115,000 $\times$ 100, specified as point A). With a blocking factor of 1, the reel will contain only 4,000,000 (40,000 $\times$ 100, point B) characters, or 65 percent less information. Variations in file capacity become less extreme when working with long records. For records of 1000 characters the capacity is approximately 15,000,000 characters, when using a blocking factor of

---

[5] Input-Output Control System (IOCS) contains two sections—a Physical IOCS section which involves reading and writing records to and from a storage device, and a Logical IOCS section which involves blocking (grouping logical records in order to create the physical record) and deblocking (making one logical record available to an operational program at a time).

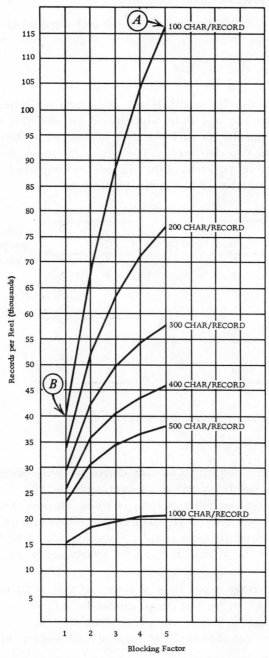

Figure 6.7. Reproduced by permission from "IBM Data File Handbook," Manual No. C20–1638, p. 25, © 1965 by International Business Machines Corporation.

119

1, compared to 21,000,000 characters on the reel when using a blocking factor of 5.

The Packing ability of the tape unit

In Figure 6.7 the bit positions for one character were shown as CBA8421.[6] There are tape units which use 9 bit positions, C01234567, which makes it possible to pack the data so that one vertical row contains not one but two characters. (The one restriction is that the data be numeric.) The bit positions of the two formats nonpacked and packed numeric for the number 53 are shown Figure 6.8.

	5	3			53	
C	0	0	odd parity	C	1	one parity bit for
0	0	0		8	0	both characters
1	0	0		4	1	
2	0	0		2	0	5
3	0	1		1	1	
4	0	0		8	0	
5	1	0		4	0	
6	0	0		2	1	3
7	0	0		1	1	
	a				b	

Figure 6.8 (a) Nonpacked numeric and (b) packed numeric.

Data Retrieval

When utilizing a sequential storage device the only efficient way of updating a file is, before processing, to sort the transactions. Transactions are records denoting activities or changes whose purpose is to update a master file. A master file is a group of records which contain status and descriptive information; for example, inventory file, payroll file, etc. Finding a record on a tape file can be schematically represented as in Fig. 6.9.

Because the average access time of a reel of tape is 1/2 the time required to read the entire reel, tapes cannot be utilized in a real-time system for storage of master files, but since they are comparatively inexpensive they can be used for logging and storing of historical information.

[6] Called 7 track tape, each row (C position, B position, etc.) is one track.

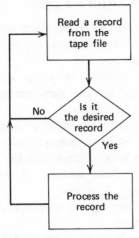

Figure 6.9

Once the analyst has obtained all the information relating to the characteristics and timings of the available units which are compatible with the previously specified computer, he can then begin determining the auxiliary data storage requirements of the system.

II. DETERMINING AUXILIARY DATA STORAGE REQUIREMENTS

On-line storage is required for many purposes. These can be categorized as follows:

A. Those requirements directly related to an application.

1. Application programs, macros, etc., needed for processing transactions, updating files and outputting of messages and reports.
2. Data records needed for the processing of transactions.
3. Tables, rates, prices, etc., required by one or more operational programs.
4. Areas reserved for future increase in the number of data records.
5. Duplicating information, duplexing, in order to reduce the duration of time that information will be unavailable because of the malfunction of a component. [Duplexing is defined as duplication of information (can also include equipment), that is used for the same purpose, in order to maintain a longer continuous period of uninterrupted service.]

B. Storage requirements for system support.

1. Computer manufacturer-supplied programs. The storage required for the operating system, line control routines, compilers, utility, and "standard" error routines.

2. Space required for storing programs and information partially processed, pre-empted by the requirements of a higher priority program (called roll-in, roll-out).

3. Queuing area(s), used to store input and output transactions. Queuing can take place in core storage. Abnormal queues, however, caused by an exceptionally large number of transactions entering the system during a short interval of time, would be stored on random access storage.

4. Space required to reconstruct information in the event of the equipment malfunction

   (a) Checkpoint—the periodic saving of key information used to continue, rather than restart, processing in the event of machine malfunction.

   (b) Logging—storing of information related to input transactions. Used for statistical purposes as well as for the reconstruction of file records in the event of a malfunction of one of the components of the system.

C. Device-dependent storage requirement. Those requirements, reviewed in Section I of this chapter, which are related to the type and electro-mechanical characteristics of the device.

1. Unusable storage, required either for the special use of computer manufacturer supplied programs or by the physical requirements of the equipment (for example, inter-record gaps, track addresses, sector constraints, designation of end of a track, etc.).

2. Indexes which are used for the accessing of information stored on random access devices.[7]

Because of the many requirements for storage, developing the file requirements of a real-time system necessitates the following:

(a) Specifying the class of devices required.

(b) Determining total random storage requirements.

(c) Ascertaining the types and number of units needed.

(d) Developing access and transfer timings.

[7] Random access and direct access are terms which are often used interchangeably. The term auxiliary storage however refers to random *and* sequential storage devices.

Specifying the Class of Devices Required

Whenever a real-time system has to process messages upon receipt, programs and data records must be *automatically* accessible to the computer. Human intervention in the normal processing of messages introduces delays which disrupt real-time processing. On-line storage is required. A device is "on-line" when it is *automatically* accessible to and under the control of the computer—that is, once real-time processing begins it is not necessary for the computer operator continuously to make data available to the computer as he would, if, for example, punched cards were the input.

There are two classes of storage whose capacity is large enough for the requirements of real-time systems—core and auxiliary storage. Though core storage, main computer memory, is available in ever-increasing sizes, in most instances it is not the cheapest device capable of doing the job. Even in its largest size it cannot provide sufficient capacity for all on-line storage requirements. The systems analyst specifying the file requirements of the system therefore must first develop a list of all storage requirements. This list must be reviewed with those who were (or are) involved with specification of the central processing unit(s), to determine

    (a) if the list of storage requirements is complete, and

    (b) which items on the list will be residing permanently in main computer memory.

For those items that will not be residing permanently in the computer memory the analyst must store the information on "slower-cheaper" devices; that is, tapes, disks, and cartridge-type units. What the systems analyst will be determining is, which is the cheapest device capable of performing in accordance with the system thruput requirements? Since tape drives are the cheapest form of auxiliary storage, the analyst should first attempt to store as much information on them as possible. The analyst must ask, "Of the items for which auxiliary storage must be provided, which should be stored on tape"? In a real-time environment, tapes are suited for storing of checkpoints, logging of processed transactions, and storing data for subsequent batch processing. The number of tape drives required is dependent upon the following:

1. Which of all the processing to be performed by the computer(s) will require the largest number of tape drives?

2. Of the information processed by the program specified in Step 1, how much of it can share the same tape drive (that is, functions requiring tape storage during different schedulable time intervals)?

3. How many drives are required by computer manufacturer-supplied routines?

Whichever answer requires the largest number of units represents the number of tape drives that will be needed. Using the five factors affecting tape capacity, discussed in Section I of this Chapter, the system analyst can then determine if there is enough on-line tape storage as well as the duration of time until each reel will exceed capacity (that is, how often will reels have to be changed). There may be items that require storage which could be stored on either tape or random access auxiliary storage. Although it would be cheaper, for example, to store some of the less frequently used operational programs on tape, this decision can be deferred until it can be determined if there will be sufficient unused random access storage. Thus, after all random access requirements have been satisfied, "border line" storage decisions can be made. The storage decisions developed thus far, that is, which items of information can be stored on tape, should now be documented and, for the time being put aside. Analysis will now continue with those items still remaining on the list—those which appear to require random access storage.

Determining Total Random Access Storage Requirements

For each class of information remaining (application and system support), an estimate of the *total* random access storage required should now be made. This is done so that the analyst need not involve himself in specifying devices for which there is insufficient capacity. For example, if total storage requirements are thirty-six million characters there is no need *at this time* to analyze storage requirements for units with capacities of two to four million characters. Thus the analyst can now determine random access storage requirements needed by each application, system support and the device themselves for units having sufficient capacity.

Application Storage Requirements

To determine storage required for each application the analyst should

    (a) obtain from the operational program development group their estimate of the size of all tables and programs that will not be permanently stored within the computer and are needed for processing transactions.

(b) review the operational program logic for the names of all files accessed by the operational programs when processing input transactions. This is necessary in order to determine the fields that will be a part of each record, as well as the number of characters contained in each field. This information should then be checked against the information, previously received, for discrepancies. If the operational logic has not been fully developed, much of this information can be obtained from the file sheets which contain information about existing manual files. If the application is presently being processed on a batch basis by a computer, a file record layout is the source for this information.

The system analyst must keep in mind that the file sheets and batch processed record layouts cannot be used verbatim, as individual files described in the file sheets often contain duplicate information. The analyst can, however, use the sheets for all of the files that will be stored on random access storage to determine those duplicated fields that can be eliminated. An example of the elimination of duplicate fields is shown in the representative Product Record (used by the Purchasing Department), Inventory Record (maintained by the Inventory Control Department) and a Pending Receipts Record (used by the Receiving Department). The fields of each of these records have been listed in Table 6.3.

The three records presently contain twenty-nine fields with a total of 233 characters. These records can be combined and duplicate fields can be eliminated which reduces the total number of fields to 19 saving 87 characters. (Fields 13, 14, 22, 23, 24, 25, 26, 27, 28, and 29 appear more than once.) Blindly combining records to eliminate duplicate fields may create more problems than it solves. Therefore, the analyst must consider the following:

1. Would the combined record be of such a size that it would create a storage problem for main memory?
2. Are the fields required for related transactions; that is, if the record were not combined, would multiple reads be required?
3. Does the system appear to be I-O bound? In such a situation combining records could reduce thruput by requiring more information to be brought into the computer than is needed for the processing of a single transaction.
4. Will the combined record exceed the maximum length that can be brought into core storage by one read instruction?

TABLE 6.3   Three File Record Layouts

Product (File) Record		Inventory (File) Record		Pending Receipts (File) Record	
Name of Field	No. of Char.	Name of Field	No. of Char.	Name of Field	No. of Char.
1. Product number	8	13. Product number	8	23. Purchase order number	6
2. Product description	21	14. Product description	21	24. Date ordered	6
3. Supplier number	10	15. Storage location	5	25. Supplier name	15
4. Supplier name	15	16. Total quant. on hand	8	26. Supplier number	10
5. Purchase order no.	6	17. Total quant. ordered	7	27. Quant. ordered	7
6. Quant. on order	7	18. Reserved on hand	7	28. Storeroom location	5
7. Unit of order	2	19. Balance	7	29. Date shipment to arrive	6
8. Unit price	6	20. Minimum supply	7		—
9. Total Price	8	21. Average usage (per month)	7	Total char. record 55	
10. Order classification code	3	22. Order classification code	3	Total of all 3 records 29 fields—233 char.	
11. Date ordered	6				
12. Date goods required	6				
	—		—		
Total char. record 98		Total char. record 80			

5. How does combining records affect the addition-deletion rate?

6. Will the length of the combined record be such that it affects the packing of the unit? If, for example, track capacity is 2000 characters, and length of the combined record is 800 characters, two records can be stored on a track with 400 unusable positions. If the record length were only 600 characters three records could fit on a track with only 200 unused positions.

7. How many records will there be in a file? The greater the number of records, the greater the number of positions of random access storage. For example, in a file with 12 duplicate characters per record and 1000 records; by combining records, 12,000 character positions can be saved. 1,200,000 positions can be saved if the file contains 100,000 records.

Summing up, it pays to combine files if

(a) there will be a reduction in the number of reads and writes required for the processing of *each* transaction using the combined file *and*

(b) it will not cause an appreciable change in the packing factor, *and*

(c) there will be a substantial saving in the amount of secondary storage required.

For the three records shown in Table 6.3 it would be advisable to combine the Product and Receipts Records, since the storage requirement will be less and, for many types of transactions, only one read and write will be required.

To the total storage requirements so far developed, space should be added (provided) for codes, miscellaneous information, and duplexing (if so decided). After estimating the changes to the total storage caused by additions and deletions, all findings should be documented. Figure 6.10, File Storage Requirements Summary Sheet, is an example of a form that can be used for the documentation of storage requirements. Information developed for the newly combined Product and Receipts File, now called the Products-Receipt File, has been entered. Further analysis is required before the sheet can be completed.

System Support Storage Requirements

The following is a list of system support functions which, if applicable, require random access storage. Along with each are the sources from which estimates of the amount of secondary storage required can be obtained.

1. Computer manufacturer-supplied programs. The obvious and most reliable source for storage size information is the computer manufacturer, since these programs were written by their staff. The exact storage requirements can be quickly ascertained.

2. Roll-in/Roll-out. The size of the area required in secondary storage can be *estimated* by determining the largest operational program to be transferred to random access storage when pre-empted by a routine of higher priority. If nested interrupts (an interrupt of an interrupt) are permitted, the size of the largest interruptable program within the number of nested interrupts times the number of permissible nested interrupts is the size of the roll-in/roll-out area. Added to this storage requirement should be a factor (15 percent for small programs, 7 or 8 percent for large routines) to provide space in the event that there is a mis-estimate as to the size of the operational program.

```
FILE STORAGE REQUIREMENTS

              SUMMARY SHEET


                                    Page    1    of _____
                                    Date:   Feb 16, 19-
                                    Analyst: J. Jones
                                    Manager:    A. Smith

A.    DATA FILE REQUIREMENTS

      1.  File Name: Products-Receipts    2.  File No.    001

      3.  Storage Device  Random Access
                                                    Index
          Access Method  ☐ Random  ☐ Sequential  ☐ Sequential
                         ☐ Other

          Sequenced by: _____

          File Duplexed:  ☐ Yes  ☑ No (If yes, show non-duplex
                                          and duplex storage req'ts)

      4.  Total Record Storage Requirements

          a.  Size of one record: 146 characters
          b.  Present total number of records: 14,000
          c.  a x b (x 2 if duplexed) = 2,044,000 characters

          List (or layout) of all fields attached:  ☐ Yes  ☑ No

          Names (numbers) of programs using this file:

                  Receipts Inquiry Routine (program number not as yet
                  assigned)

                            %     %      Net % increase Year   If duplexing
                                                                 applicable
          Total Storage: Add. Del.     +10 This year, 19__ x 2 = _____
                                       +10 Next year, 19__ x 2 = _____
                                       +10 Third year, 19__ x 2 = _____
                                       +10 4th year, 19__ x 2 = _____
                                       +10    year, 19__ x 2 = _____
                                       ___    year, 19__ x 2 = _____

B.    OTHER REQUIREMENTS (for this data file)

      1.     Indexes           _____
      2.     Data Records      _____
      3.     Overflow Average  _____
      4.     Waste Storage     _____
      +4c above                _____


                    Total      _____


      Assigned to (Location/Drive) _____

      Remarks:
```

Figure 6.10

3. Work and buffer areas. These areas in core storage, reserved for blocking and deblocking, are utilized by operational programs. In the event that a program is rolled out, the work and buffer areas must also be written on random access storage. The estimated size of these areas can be obtained from the analysts that developed the operational program logic.
4. Message queuing. When the input and output areas are full with real-time messages the logic of the real-time system may be designed so that messages are temporarily stored on a random access device. The amount of storage required for this is the maximum number of characters physically possible to transmit per second, times the number of seconds that it is desirable to accept input at a rate faster than it can be processed. There could be two queue areas, one for unprocessed input messages and another for output transactions.

If the maximum number of characters that could enter the system in a second has not yet been ascertained (the terminal and line analysis had not begun) an estimate of the total number of characters to be queued can be made [the number of characters per second times the estimated number of communication lines times the maximum period of permissible queuing (before the terminals are not permitted to enter data) equals the amount of random access storage required]. The analyst should make a note to review this assumption, the number of lines, and the character transfer rate, once the terminal and line analysis is completed.

Ascertaining the Types and Number of Units Needed

Once the random access requirements have been estimated, the analyst can make a preliminary specification of equipment. From his list of random access devices with sufficient capacity he must find those that are compatible with, and can be attached to, the computer that has been specified. If, for example, estimated total on-line storage requirements developed so far was 17,600,000 characters, the types of devices that either individually or in combination would provide sufficient storage consist of:

(a) 1 25-million character device, rental $1,700 per month;
(b) 2 11-million character devices, rental $1,400 per month;
(c) 2 8-million character devices and, 1 3-million character device providing 19,000,000 character total storage at a, rental $1,900 per month; and
(d) 2 8-million character devices and 1 2-million character device,

supplying 18 million positions of storage, rental $1,800 per month.

Note: The rental of the control units for the four alternatives should be kept in mind as costs now become a factor in the selection of devices.

The reasoning involved in selecting one of the four choices could be as follows. Alternative (a) can be eliminated, since even when operational program storage is included over 7 million positions of storage would remain unused. The capacity provided with Alternative (d) leaves insufficient storage for record identifiers (keys), gaps, and alternate track addresses as well as for unforseen deviations from previous file requirement estimates. Alternatives (b) and (c) remain, and of the two, (b) becomes the first choice because of its cost. Alternative (c), at this stage of the analysis, appears to offer only increased cost. All of these alternatives are still held in reserve in the event that changes to configuration have to be made; for example, the storage device is not fast enough, more random access storage is required, or, in the unlikely event of the system having been overdesigned, less storage is needed. Since Alternative (b) provides sufficient storage for the storage of "border line" information, a decision can be made that the less frequently used operational programs can be stored on a random access device.

Developing access and transfer timings

A detailed study of the selected random access devices must now be made. In addition to learning the physical characteristics of the device, the following information should be obtained:

1. The data record capability of each track [data record capacity—physical capacity of the track—space required for record recognition (keys)—space required by the device (gaps, markers, and track addresses)].

2. The number of tracks per cylinder and per unit.

3. Distribution of seek times, including average seek time. Some random access devices do not have a standard unit of time for the movement of the read-write access mechanism from one track (or cylinder) to the next. For these devices, seek time varies depending upon the number of tracks being transversed.

4. Average access time.

5. Character transfer rate.

6. Special features, such as the ability to pack numeric data, read-release feature, search in channel, etc.

Using this information, the analyst can determine the number of records that can be stored in each unit. Given the length of each logical record, a formula, and/or table is available to show the number of records and the amount of unusable storage for various blocking factors. By using the track device capacities of the IBM 2311 shown in Table 6.4,[9] the analyst can determine the number of records per track for a file organization requiring keys. Given a data file with records of 109 characters in length, 18 unblocked records can be stored on one track. (Actually, the record length could vary from 109 to 119 characters and 18 records could still fit on one track.) 180 records could be stored in one cylinder and 36,000 records could be accommodated in one pack. Unavailable storage could be determined as follows: track capacity obtained from the device manual is 3605 characters. 1962 character positions, eighteen 109-character unblocked records represent used storage. 3605 minus 1962 or 1643 character positions represents unusable data record storage for unblocked records. Space in core storage and transfer time permitting records can be blocked. If 541 positions of core storage could be made available, 4 blocks of 6 records each, or 24 records in all, could be stored on one track. Unusable storage would then be only 989 positions per track, 3605−(109 × 24), and the total capacity of the cylinder and pack would be increased to 240 records (40 blocks × 6 records/block) and 48,000 characters (8000 blocks × 6 records/block) records respectively. Note from the table that if the size of the record could be reduced by packing or some other record compacting technique to 106 characters, 5 blocks of 6 records each would fit on one track. Unusable storage would be reduced to 425 positions per track, 3605−(106 × 30) while cylinder and pack capacity would now be 300 (50 blocks × 6 records/block) records per cylinder and 60,000 (10,000 blocks × 6 records/block) records per pack.

For those who prefer using a formula,[9] the number of records that can be stored on one 2311 track is equal to

$$1 + \frac{3625 - (20 - C + KL + DL)}{81 - C + 1.049\,(KL + DL)}$$

Where
$KL =$ Key length
$DL =$ Length of data record
$C = 0$

[9] IBM, "IBM Data File Handbook," Manual No. C20-1638, p. 39.

● WITH KEYS

BYTES PER RECORD		RECORDS PER			TRANSMISSION TIME IN MS PER RECORD	
MINIMUM	MAXIMUM	TRACK	CYLINDER	MODULE	MINIMUM	MAXIMUM
1721	3605	1	10	2000	11.03	23.11
1112	1720	2	20	4000	7.13	11.03
812	1111	3	30	6000	5.21	7.12
633	811	4	40	8000	4.06	5.20
513	632	5	50	10000	3.29	4.05
429	512	6	60	12000	2.75	3.28
365	428	7	70	14000	2.34	2.74
316	364	8	80	16000	2.03	2.33
276	315	9	90	18000	1.77	2.02
245	275	10	100	20000	1.57	1.76
218	244	11	110	22000	1.40	1.56
195	217	12	120	24000	1.25	1.39
175	194	13	130	26000	1.12	1.24
159	174	14	140	28000	1.02	1.12
144	158	15	150	30000	0.92	1.01
131	143	16	160	32000	0.84	0.92
120	130	17	170	34000	0.77	0.83
109	119	18	180	36000	0.70	0.76
100	108	19	190	38000	0.64	0.69
91	99	20	200	40000	0.58	0.63
83	90	21	210	42000.	0.53	0.58
77	82	22	220	44000	0.49	0.53
70	76	23	230	46000	0.45	0.49
64	69	24	240	48000	0.41	0.44
59	63	25	250	50000	0.38	0.40
54	58	26	260	52000	0.35	0.37
49	53	27	270	54000	0.31	0.34
45	48	28	280	56000	0.29	0.31
41	44	29	290	58000	0.26	0.28
37	40	30	300	60000	0.24	0.26
34	36	31	310	62000	0.22	0.23
30	33	32	320	64000	0.19	0.21
27	29	33	330	66000	0.17	0.19
24	26	34	340	68000	0.15	0.17
21	23	35	350	70000	0.13	0.15
19	20	36	360	72000	0.12	0.13
17	18	37	370	74000	0.11	0.12
14	16	38	380	76000	0.09	0.10
12	13	39	390	78000	0.08	0.08
9	11	40	400	80000	0.06	0.07
7	8	41	410	82000	0.04	0.05
5	6	42	420	84000	0.03	0.04

TABLE 6.4   ● WITH KEYS

* Reproduced by permission from IBM, "IBM System/360 Disk Storage Drive-Capacity and Transmission Time Reference Card," Form No. X20-1705.

Given that KL $=$ 10 and DL $=$ 109, the number of records that can be stored on one track is

$$1 + \frac{3625 - (20 - 0 + 10 + 109)}{81 - 0 + 1.049\,(10 + 109)} = 1 + \frac{3625 - 139}{81 + 124} = 1 + \frac{3486}{205} = 18$$

Thus, 18 records can fit on one track.

The records developed for the Products—Receipts File (see Table 6.3) are 153 characters each. A blocking factor of 5 was based on storage availability specified by the operational program logic development group and is an attempt to balance storage utilization with Input-Output record transfer times. A 765 (153 $\times$ 5) character block permits 4 blocks, or 20 records, per track. Since there are an estimated 14,000 records, 700 tracks (70 cylinders) will be required for this file. Similarly, the number of tracks needed for all of the data records, programs, queries, etc. must be ascertained.

The selection of an access method must now be made. If the Products —Receipts File will be accessed by means of indexes, there will be, in all probability, one index entry for each track. The number of tracks required for the storing of indexes can thus be determined. If, because of the space required for keys, gaps, etc. the total number of tracks required exceeds the number available (or the types and number of devices specified) a change in the original device configuration will have to be made. If different types of devices are specified all previous storage estimates, blocking, etc. may have to be redone for the new device(s). If reanalysis is not required, or has been completed, access and transfer times can be determined for each file of data record, programs, and tables. At this stage of the system design average timings are sufficient. The "average time" is the interval of time starting from the beginning of the execution of the seek until the checking of the last character transferred into core storage.[10] For the reading of records, this average time consists of: a seek, rotational delay, read indexes, search indexes, switch read-write heads to track containing the record, rotational delay, and reading the data.

For writing a record the seek time is 0 ms. *if* the arm has been held to write a record that has just been read into core storage. The execution of the work command causes the following to take place: rotational delay, write, rotational delay, and write check. Write check is the verification that the information was written correctly onto the random access device. The time required to read and write is a function of the number of

[10] Waits and delays caused by other transactions would not be included.

characters being transferred. In the example shown in Table 6.5, transmission time was computed by multiplying the minimum and maximum bytes per record by 0.00064193, the time in milliseconds (specified by the manufacturer of the device) required by the equipment to transfer one character from the disk surface into core storage or vice versa. Using the average seek time, 85 ms., and a rotational delay time of 12.5 ms. the time required for reading and writing one 153 character record would be:

TABLE 6.5

For Reading a Record		For Writing a Record	
Seek time	85.0 ms.	Seek time	0 ms.
Rotational delay	12.5 "	Rotational delay	12.5 "
Read ½ track of indexes	12.5 "	Write record	5.1 "
Search indexes (no computer time		Rotational delay for write check	
if an in-channel search)	0 "	25 − 4. ms. =	20.3 "
Switch read/write mechanism	0 "	Write check	5.1 "
Rotational delay	12.5 "		
Read the data record (153 char.			
record × 5 records/block			
× 0.9064193 = 5.0107635) or	5.1 "		
Total	**127.6 ms.**	**Total**	**43.0 ms.**

Carrying Table 6.5 further, if the main processing time was 20 ms. and initial processing was 5 ms., the total processing time for this transaction (excluding IOCS and operating system execution time) would be:

1. Initial processing — 5.0 ms.
2. Read data record from Product File — 127.6 ms.
3. Main processing — 20.0 ms.
4. Write the updated record back onto disk storage — 43.0 ms.

Total — 195.6 ms.

Total time is less than ⅕th of a second. Approximately 81 percent of this time, however, is I-O time. Reading and writing consisted of only 15.3 ms.; 8.3 percent of the I-O time is used for transferring the record.

Once these times have been calculated for each file, the rest of the file storage requirements summary sheet should be filled out, copied, and given to the operational program development group for inclusion with the total processing time.

Before analysis of file requirements can be considered to be complete, specifications for file feedback must be developed.

SPECIFICATION OF FILE FEEDBACK

Many assumptions are made when determining the file requirements for the system. A combination of mis-estimates and/or modifications can create a situation in which the system could not function. Advanced knowledge of their effect on the system would permit careful planning as to how to modify the system. As far as files are concerned, the following information is important:

1. The rate of change of the size of each file. A count of all additions and deletions to the file should be recorded. After a period of time a trend will become evident. Projection of this trend will tell the analyst at what point he must increase, or change, his random access configuration. It is the increasing trend that is of most concern to the analyst, if for no other reason than the time it takes for a computer manufacturer to fill an order for additional random access equipment.

2. The number of overflow records. Every time an overflow record must be accessed, additional time, extra rotational delay, as well as an additional read is required to transfer a record into computer memory. If the file is not periodically resequenced the average time to process a record will increase. Keeping track of the number of records stored in the overflow area will, once a decision is made as to how many overflow records will be permitted prior to re-sequencing the file, signal when the file should be resequenced, and eliminate the situation of having no space on overflow areas.

3. The number of file updates. Keeping track of the number of times records are updated can be used to set the interval of time when the file should be copied or dumped. A file is periodically dumped in order to reduce the time required to reconstruct the file. Whenever a disk unit malfunctions or invalid information is encountered on the file, part or all of the file must be reconstructed. Reconstruction consists of using the last copy of the file, and updating it with the transactions that have been logged. By setting the point at which the file will be duplicated the maximum time (maximum number of transactions required to update the file) will be known.

These controls may be established by specifying

(a) that every time a record is added to or removed from the file, a special record or field in the data record that keeps count of these changes is updated;

(b) a routine to scan, count, and print the number of records in each overflow area; and

(c) a program to scan the transaction log and count the number of times each file has been updated, thus keeping track of file activity for purpose of dumping.

Completion of the documentation of all findings and assumptions, as well as the specification of feedback controls triggers a review of the file analysis by the project manager. Unless changes are required, either because of results obtained from simulation or changes to specifications, specification of the file requirements can be considered complete.

CONCLUSION

The steps for determining the file requiremnts of the system can be summarized as follows:

1. Determine (list) all storage requirements.
2. Determine those items which will permanently reside in main computer memory.
3. For the remaining items determine the cheapest class of device on which information can be stored.
4. For those which can be stored on sequential storage (tape) determine
   (a) the number of drives required, and
   (b) the maximum amount of data that can be stored on each reel and estimated interval of processing time until each reel will exceed capacity.
5. Document all analyses that relates to those items which will be stored on tapes.
6. Determine which items can be stored on either sequential or random access storage.
7. For remaining items requiring random access storage, estimate total storage required.
8. Select those units wihch appear to have sufficient capacity.
9. Determine application storage requirements by
   (a) Ascertaining the size of all tables, sub-routines, and programs which will be transferred (on demand) into computer storage,
   (b) Using the operational program logic as a guide to determine the fields that will comprise each type of file record.
   (c) Providing auxiliary storage for miscellaneous information, codes, etc., as well as for the duplexing of any of the data files
10. Determine the amount of auxiliary storage needed for system support (computer manufacturer supplied programs) work areas, and message queuing.

11. Select those auxiliary storage units capable of storing all the on-line random access requirements of the system.
12. Determine the number of records that can be stored on each unit by assigning locations to each of the items/files requiring random access storage. If there appears to be a minimum of unused storage available, transfer some of the files that can be stored on either sequential or random access storage to sequential devices.
13. Calculate record access and transfer timings.
14. Specify file feedback requirements.
15. Document all analysis.

CHAPTER 7

Specification of Terminal, Line and Control Unit Requirements

REAL-TIME SYSTEMS HAVE INCREASED THE VARIETY AND NUMBER OF INPUT AND OUTPUT DEVICES WHICH PERMIT THE AUTOMATIC TRANSFER OF DATA, REGARDLESS OF PHYSICAL LOCATION. SPECIFICATION OF EQUIPMENT NEEDED FOR THE IMMEDIATE TRANSFER OF INFORMATION IS REVIEWED IN THIS CHAPTER.

I. CONCEPTS AND TERMS

In a real-time system the transfer of information from remote locations into a computer differs from the movement of data from auxiliary storage devices:

1. A message can be transferred from a remote location in sections with checking taking place after each part.
2. A request to send data can originate at the remote location, whereas a request for data from an auxiliary storage device is initiated only by the computer.

Two of the components involved in the transfer of data in a real-time system are terminals and communication lines. These in turn constitute a network. A terminal is a device that accepts keyed or punched data as input to send to the computer and/or produces printed, punched, visually displayed data, or audio messages as output (from the computer). Each terminal is called a component, and all the components at one location are called a station (or terminal station).

Figure 7.1 is an example of a typewriter, used as an input and output device. It is used when a paper (hard) copy of inputs and/or outputs is required.

Figure 7.2, an on-line card reader, is used when there is a need to input constant information. This type of data can be prepunched in order to reduce the time and amount of information to be entered via a slower keyboard.

138

Figure 7.1 An IBM 1050 typewriter terminal.

A communication line (also called a channel or circuit) is a path for electrical transmission between a terminal(s) and a computer and consists of a group of wires or a special part of the radio frequency spectrum.

A network is the interconnection of terminal stations and communication lines with a computer(s) for the purpose of transferring/processing information. Figure 7.3, a schematic of a communication network connected to a real-time system, shows four different types of lines.

Lines A and E are examples of point-to-point transmission. Point-to-point transmission is any connection between two terminals or between a terminal and a computer.

Line C in Figure 7.3 is a multipoint line. A multipoint line contains more than one terminal station on one communication line. Note however that the connection between T.S.-A and T.S.-B is a point-to-point connection.

Line B consists of four multipoint lines entering a line concentrator. A line concentrator is a device which accepts data from many low speed, low activity stations (generally situated near each other) and transfers these data to the computer at higher speeds. It is capable of reversing this function as well—that is, it receives data from the computer at a faster rate than it sends it to the terminal stations by storing the data temporarily in its own buffer memory. This technique is utilized to reduce line costs.

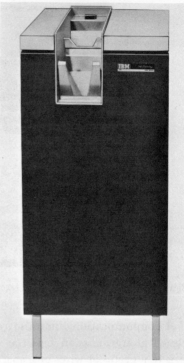

Figure 7.2 An IBM 1056 card reader terminal.

Line *D* is a dial-up or switched line which can be used when terminal stations have limited data transmission requirements. A telephone connection is made, temporarily connecting the terminal directly to the computer. When all transmissions are completed, the terminal is disconnected from the computer. This technique also reduces line costs since the user is charged only for the duration of the connection.

Regardless of the type of connection there are three types of lines: *simplex, half-duplex* and *full-duplex*. A simplex line can transmit data in one direction only—that is, *either* to or from the computer. A half-duplex line can transfer information in either direction, to or from the computer, but only in one direction at a time. Changing transmission from one direction to another is called "turning the line around," and is accomplished by a Line Control Unit. This Line Control Unit can be a simple data exchange, or—a multiplexor. As a multiplexor it can be connected to a computer or can stand alone, working as a special purpose computer. A full-duplex line can transfer data simultaneously in two directions to *and* from the computer. A full-duplex line consists of two simplex lines—one attached to an output component, the other to an input.

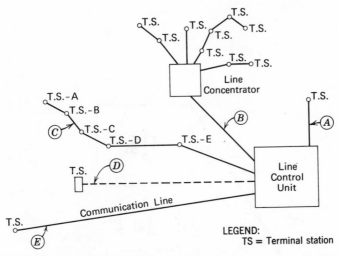

Figure 7.3 A real-time communication network.

The rate at which a line is able to transfer data is referred to as "the speed of the line." Line speeds are often divided into four major categories, or grades: teletype, subvoice grade, voice grade, and broad band. The speed of each are as follows:

Grade of Line	Line Speed (approximate)
1. Teletype	45 to 75 bits per second
2. Sub voice grade	150 to 600 bits per second
3. Voice grade	2400 bits per second
4. Broad band	Related to the width of the band [1] (Microwave)

Various line speeds are provided for devices capable of receiving information at that rate. A balance is obtained when the speed at which a device is able to transmit (send or receive) information is equal to the speed of the line.

Information may pass through several different types of equipment before it reaches its final destination. Line E in Figure 7.3 has been enlarged in Figure 7.4 to show the equipment required for transfers of information. The same equipment would be required for a multipoint line.

For a dial-up transmission, telephones would be required at point F and in most instances point G as well.

---

[1] One type of broad band channel that was used for core-to-core transmission was capable of transmitting 5,100 characters (35,000+) bits per second.

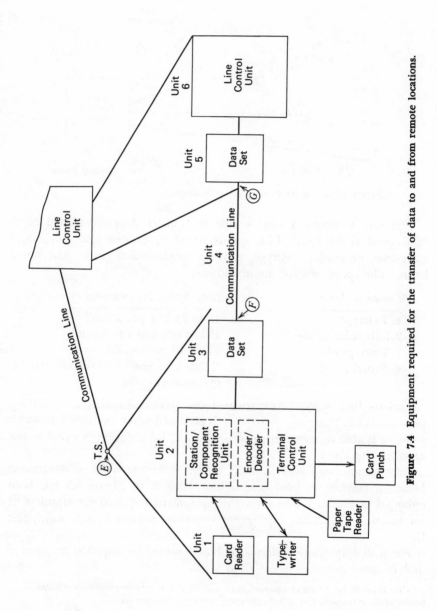

Figure 7.4 Equipment required for the transfer of data to and from remote locations.

The purpose of each device shown in Figure 7.4, can be summarized as follows:

Unit 1—the terminal may be a card reader, printer, typewriter, card punch, etc. It is the origin of the information (if the component is an input unit) or the destination of the data (if the device is an output unit).

Unit 2—the terminal control unit serves the following three functions:

(a) Conversion of the code of the terminal into one which can be transmitted to a computer. For messages being received from a computer it must change the code to the one used by the output device. This function is accomplished by the "Encoder/Decoder."

(b) Station and component recognition. Hardware is incorporated within the terminal control unit so that it is able to recognize a signal sent from the Line Control Unit. This recognition is needed so that the correct component on a multipoint line receives the message. In addition the control unit is capable of routing the signal (message) to the correct component. Component and station identification codes are set by engineers when installing the terminals.

(c) Assembling-Disbursing of data. A communication line transfers information serially by bit. When data is sent to one of the components attached to the terminal control unit, bits must be collected, assembled into characters, and the characters transferred to the prespecified output device. For messages being sent to the computer, the terminal control unit accepts the characters from the device and sends them to the Line Control Unit via a data set, one bit at a time.

Data sets, Units 3 and 5 in Figure 7.4, convert bits into signals which can be transmitted across communication lines. When receiving information data sets convert signals into bits.

Unit 4—the communication line is used for the transmission of data. When traveling across communication lines, a bit and no-bit condition are signals. They vary in level of transmitted energy by a prespecified amount.

Figure 7.5 is a schematic of a "1 0 1 0 0" bit transmission occurring in five time units. Information is transmitted across communication lines in one of three ways:

1. Start-Stop Transmission. In front of each group of bits representing one character is a special bit—a start bit. At the end of each

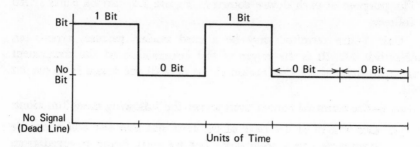

Figure 7.5

character is a bit of a different length than the standard bit time. Certain types of telegraph and typewriter devices use 1.42 bit times for the designation of a stop bit. Thus if a character contains 7 bit positions, 7 bit times + the additional time required for the start and stop bits are transmitted. Start-Stop is also known as asynchronous transmission.

2. Synchronous Transmission. This is transmission without start or stop bits. The sending and receiving devices are first synchronized with each other by means of a special bit pattern. This special pattern is regenerated periodically to keep the sending and receiving devices in unison. Synchronization coordinates the *time* that the receiving device will begin collecting (sampling) for bit or no-bit patterns with the time that the sending unit begins transmitting. With this technique, 7 bit positions will take only 7 bit times to transmit—a substantial saving in productive transmission time.

3. Parallel Transmission. By using one transmission line for each bit position a character can be transferred in parallel. Thus a 7 bit position character requires 7 channels to transmit.

Unit 6—the Line Control Unit, controls and coordinates the flow of information to and from terminal stations. Depending on the unit, functions performed include the following:

1. Code conversion—changing the signals sent by the terminal control unit into computer intelligible codes.

2. Assemble bits into characters.

3. Send and receive signals from/to terminal stations.

4. Check incoming messages for correct transmissions.

5. Insertion of functional characters on outgoing messages. A functional character is made a part of a message in order to ensure

proper transmission. The carriage return key on a typewriter, End of Message, and LRC (Longitudinal Redundancy Check) are examples of functional characters.

6. Elimination of functional characters from incoming messages.

These functions are similar to those performed by a terminal control unit. A Line Control Unit, however, monitors the entire network on an active basis whereas a terminal control unit services the components at a single station. The three major types of Line Control Units are shown in Table 1, along with the advantages and disadvantages of each.

Most real-time systems use a main computer plus a data exchange or multiplexor for the control of the flow of information to and from the terminals. Polling is the most common technique employed to coordinate and control this function regardless of the type of line control unit. With a multiplexor, polling is initiated and controlled by a multiplexor unit, and with a data exchange this is a function of the main computer. When polling, the computer system interrogates each station on each line, asking if

(a) there are data to be transferred to the computer (for input devices) and

(b) the terminal is able to receive information (for output devices)

It should be noted that polling and/or the transfer of data can take place simultaneously on *each* communication line.

The sequence in which terminal stations are interrogated (polled) is specified by means of a list (called polling list). In Figure 7.3, line C has 5 stations on the same line, labelled T.S.-A through T.S.-E. A polling list for this line is A2, B2, A2, C2, D2, B2, E2. The first position, the letter, is for selection of the station, the second, the number, for the component. Assuming component 2 is a terminal reader, this list is used to interrogate the card reader at T.S.-A. If no data are to be sent to the line the computer automatically polls T.S.-B. A negative response (no data) at B will cause the next station on the list to be polled, T.S.-A again. The polling list for this line has been specified in this manner so that T.S.-A and -B will be polled twice as often as the rest of the stations on that line. This technique is used when some of the stations on a line have more data to send than others. By polling the higher volume stations more often they are given more opportunity to send data as information can only be transferred if the station is first polled.

Contention is another method of initiating data transfers. In a contention system whenever a station seizes the line (presses the Send Key)

TABLE 7.1

Type	Advantages	Disadvantages
A. Control Unit (Data exchange/transmission control unit).	1. Transfers line status, control and assembly of bits into characters	1. Data can be lost if not transferred from buffers in the core in sufficient time. 2. Increased number of interrupts during transfer of data to the main computer. Some types of data exchanges will trigger an interrupt every time the buffer is full. The buffers are limited as to the number of characters they can hold. 3. Most of the line control functions, listed previously, are performed by the main computer, thus increasing processing time.
B. Special purpose programmable computer (multiplexor, attached to a General Purpose Computer).	1. Capable of performing code conversion. 2. Formatting messages for output from and input to the main computer by inserting/stripping off functional characters. 3. Queuing large numbers of messages, transferred at high speed to main computer. 4. Initiating polling; maintain line status.	1. Increases cost of equipment. 2. Programming multiplexors require special training.
C. Main computer with full line control capabilities (stand along multiplexor).	1. Reduced hardware cost as separate equipment to perform these functions is not required.	1. Increases processing time as regular processing plus all line control functions are accomplished by one machine.

it locks out (prevents) all other stations on that line from sending until it is finished.

Because each transmission line operates independently and simultaneously with the other lines of the network, a strict discipline must be adhered to in the transfer of data across communication lines. An example of the sequence of events involved in a transfer of data in a multipoint polling system using half-duplex lines is shown in Figure 7.6.

The steps shown combine the interaction of programming and mechanically initiated actions.

COMMON CARRIERS

While computers, files, and terminal equipment can be obtained from computer manufacturers, communication facilities are supplied by *common carriers*. These companies are licensed by the FCC (Federal Communications Commission) to supply communication services. American Telephone and Telegraph Company (AT&T), General Telephone and Electronics Corporation, Western Union Telegraph Company, Radio Corporation of America Communications, Inc., American Cable and Radio Corporation, plus over 2,800 independently owned telephone companies supply the United States with communication services. Common carrier charges for communication services are called tariffs (charges and rates for usage) and have been filed with and approved by the FCC. Tariffs are based on distance (miles of lines used), the number of hours services are required, and the time of the day when these services will be used, as well as the type and transfer rate of the lines. Charges for the number of miles of communication lines used are determined by measuring all distances according to the "V-H Coordinate Measuring Plan." Maps of the United States and Canada have been subdivided into many vertical and horizontal parallel lines, similar to those for longitudes and latitudes, with a number assigned to each line. Using a system of triangulation, one can determine the distance between any two geographical locations easily, quickly, and accurately.

Communication charges are also affected by the number of hours. Special "pricing packages" are available to heavy users of communication services. Telpak, Multiple Channel Pricing, and WATS are names of three "pricing packages."

II. SPECIFICATIONS OF COMMUNICATION REQUIREMENTS

The methods used to determine the communication requirements of the system can be summarized as follows. First the terminals to be used are specified. By using the maximum number of transactions entering the system in a given interval of time and the time required to enter manually one message, determining the number of terminals required is basically a matter of arithmetic. For example, if 60 messages are expected to enter and/or leave the system in a ten-minute interval occurring during the peak period, and two minutes are required to

COMMENTS

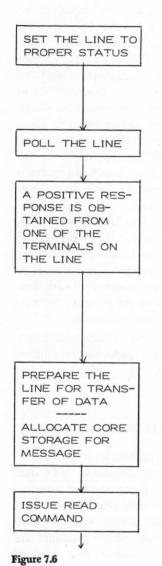

SET THE LINE TO PROPER STATUS

The status of each line must be changed (set) for each function -- polling as well as the sending and receiving of data. Polling of each terminal (on several or all lines simultaneously) takes place in accordance with the sequence specified in the polling list for each line

POLL THE LINE

A POSITIVE RESPONSE IS OBTAINED FROM ONE OF THE TERMINALS ON THE LINE

A positive response (i.e. there is data to be sent into the computer) identifying the line and the terminal wishing to send a message to the computer.   A negative response indicates that the terminal is either not in the ready status or that it has no data to send, resulting in the continuation of polling.   An operator, when having data to send, depresses the enter or request key.   It is the depression of this key that results in a positive response when the ready terminal is polled.

PREPARE THE LINE FOR TRANSFER OF DATA

ALLOCATE CORE STORAGE FOR MESSAGE

The line is changed into receive status. A message (start transmission) is sent to proper terminal.   All other terminals on that line are prevented from sending or receiving signals (locked out).   The location in computer/multiplex memory into which the data will be read has been reserved and specified to the control unit.

ISSUE READ COMMAND

Transfer of data into computer/multiplexor memory begins

Figure 7.6

148

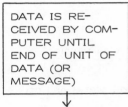

```
┌─────────────────┐
│ DATA IS RE-     │
│ CEIVED BY COM-  │
│ PUTER UNTIL     │
│ END OF UNIT OF  │
│ DATA (OR        │
│ MESSAGE)        │
└─────────────────┘
        ↓
```

DATA
TRANSFERRED
CORRECTLY
(A VALID
    TRANSFER)

A valid transfer is represented as number of bits sent to computer. This number is generated at terminal control unit and sent to the computer/LCU.

```
        ↓
┌─────────────────┐
│ POSSIBLE ACTION │
│ TO A VALID      │
│ TRANSFER:       │
│ 1. RESET LINE   │
│    TO POLL      │
│ 2. PUT LINE IN  │
│    HOLD STATUS  │
│    FOR OUTPUT   │
│    MESSAGE      │
└─────────────────┘
```

Some programs permit continuation of polling at next terminal on polling list. Others require resetting pointers to the first terminal on the polling list as they were destroyed upon interrupt.

```
        ↓
┌─────────────────┐
│ AFTER PROCESS-  │
│ ING FORMAT      │
│ OUTPUT MESS-    │
│ AGE             │
└─────────────────┘
```

a.   Terminal line number inserted in message header
b.   Delay characters (if required) inserted
c.   Functional characters inserted
d.   Code conversion (if required)

```
        ↓
┌─────────────────┐
│ SET LINE TO     │
│ SEND STATUS     │
│ ────            │
│ ISSUE WRITE     │
│ COMMAND         │
└─────────────────┘
        ↓
```

Write command specifies location from which data is transferred to the terminal.

Figure 7.6

149

OUTPUT MESSAGE RECEIVED BY TERMINAL CORRECTLY (A VALID TRANSFER)	Total number of bits sent = to number of bits counted by the control unit of the terminal. Unequal count (error) will result in a request for retransmission.

↓

ON VALID END OF MESSAGE SIGNAL: 1. TERMINAL RELEASED 2. LINE IS RE-SET TO POLL	End of message (valid transmission) releases core used. The line is reset to poll status and pollings begin again.

Figure 7.6

transfer the message, there must be enough terminals to transfer 12 messages every two minutes. Since it takes two minutes to enter one message, 12 terminals are required.

The location of each type of terminal is determined by using the diagram of the company's facilities. Once the types of terminals are known, line requirements can be ascertained, since each type of terminal works only with one type of line. Because the number of lines required limits the range of choice of the Line Control Unit, it is the last component to be specified.

Specification of communication equipment can begin once the following are available:

1. The list of transactions with their associate anticipated volumes that will be transferred on a real-time basis.

2. The size of each field of each transaction. This information was developed from the message sheets filled out during the study of present procedures.

3. Information concerning the types, costs, and characteristics of available (standard) terminals, lines, and control units compatible with the previously specified Central Processor(s).

4. A drawing showing the location of all departments, offices, personnel, desks, and files.

5. Specification of the line control program(s) support provided by the computer manufacturer.

By using this information, we can specify the equipment required for on-line data transfers: the terminals, the communication lines, and the controlling units as follows:

(a) Specify message formats.
(b) Determine the location of all terminals.
(c) Ascertain the number of terminals needed at each location.
(d) Specify the communication network.
(e) Determine type and number of line control unit(s).

SPECIFY MESSAGE FORMATS

The time required to transfer a message to or from a terminal is a function of the number of characters entering the system. The analyst must analyze each message of each application and determine the minimum, average, and maximum number of characters in each message. Figure 7.7 is a sample of a form that can be used to organize information concerning the size of each message. Note that space is provided for the functional characters required by the terminal. The number of characters to be added to the message is obtained from specifications issued by the manufacturer of the terminal. Functional characters should be added during the specification of terminals since it varies for each type of terminal device.

DETERMINE THE LOCATION OF ALL TERMINALS

When deciding at which point information is to enter the system via a terminal, the analyst should try to enter data as close to their origin as possible.

Example: For a savings account application, should the transaction enter the computer system at the time the amount deposited is entered in a deposit book; or should information be entered manually into a deposit book, then on an account card and then into the computer via a terminal? The better solution is the one that transfers as much work as possible from human beings to a computer. Using the drawing that shows the location of all departments, the analyst should make a list of all people, with their physical location, who will need some type of input terminal for entering information *into* the system. Figure 7.8 is an example of a worksheet that can be used.

This initial listing is compiled by application. The column labeled Response Required for this message (YES-NO) serves only as a preliminary indication that an output device is required at that location. The output message number will be added to the Input Terminal Worksheet, as it is a cross-reference to this list of output messages. Figure 7.9 shows the format of the Output Terminal Worksheet.

This list is developed by determining those locations that will receive the information FROM the computer system. Note that *several* locations can receive outputs triggered by a single input and that output mes-

REAL-TIME TRANSACTION SHEET NO __/2__   INPUT MSG ☑   Date: __1/16/-__
                                                OUTPUT MSG ☐   Page No.: __/2__

Application: __Inventory Control__

Message Name: __Receipt of goods from outside sources__   Message No. __I00/2__

Message Received From: __Receiving Dept.__   Terminal Device: __Typewriter__
Message to be sent to: __Storeroom__

TOTAL NUMBER OF MESSAGES OF THIS TYPE: 230

MISC:

Field No.	Field Contains	No. Char	Percent Occurrence	A/N	Comments
1	Transaction I. D.	3	100	A	
2	Purchase Order No.	8	100	A/N	
3	Quantity	4	100	N	missing if our
4	Inventory Number	7	80	A/N	copy of P.O. is not included with the B/L
5	Vendor Code No.	6	100	N	
6	Date Received	6	100	N	

Insert Delay Characters After __N/A__ Data Characters

Insert Line Shift Characters __/__ Times

No. Of Characters Required For Trans. Iden.: __3__ Keyed In __3__ Automatically Generated

No. Of Characters Required End of Message: __—__ Keyed In __3__ Automatically Generated

Analyst: __A. Allen__

Figure 7.7. Note that it is helpful to prefix all input message numbers with an "I," output message numbers with an "O."

INPUT TERMINAL WORKSHEET

Date: _1/26/–_

Application: _Inventory Control_ Analyst: _a. allen_

Message No.	Message Name	At Location	By Worker (Job Title)	Response Required Yes/No	Msg. No.	SOP Msg No.	Comments
I0012	Receipt of goods from outside sources	Receiving Dept.	Receiving Clerk	yes	00014	—	new msg type
I0013	Returns	Receiving Dept.	Returns Clerk	yes	00015	—	" "

Figure 7.8

sages can be sent automatically to locations. The input message could have been originated at some other location, or automatically triggered by the computer.

Using the Input and the Output Terminal Worksheet, the Terminal Location Worksheet, Figure 7.10, can now be filled out.

When entering information to specify the number of transactions expected during the *peak period,* the analyst should be aware if there are two peak periods, and this, along with the number of transactions an-

OUTPUT TERMINAL WORKSHEET

Date: _1/29/–_

Application: _Inventory Control_ Analyst: _a. allen_

Msg No;	Message Name	At Location	By Worker (Job Title)	Input Msg No (Triggering This Message)	Comments
00014	Acknowledgment of Receipt of goods	Receiving Dept	Receiving Clerk	I 0012	
00015	Acknowledgment of Returns	"	Return Clerk	I 0013	
00016	Movement Notice	Storeroom	Records Clerk	I 0012	Automatically sent to storeroom notifying them of a pending arrival of goods

Figure 7.9

ticipated, should be noted in the comments section of the form. The transactions listed on the Real-Time Transaction Sheets (Figure 7.7) should be used as a checklist to ensure that no messages have been overlooked when filling out the Terminal Location Worksheet.

ASCERTAIN THE NUMBER AND TYPE OF TERMINALS NEEDED AT EACH LOCATION

A complete list of terminals usable as inputs to a real-time system could consist of many devices. They can, however, be grouped as to

(a) speed of the line that can be attached to the unit,
(b) direction of the device (terminals are either input, output, or input-output devices), and
(c) the type of media produced by (or in the case of input devices—transferred from) the terminal.

For *each location* requiring a terminal (either input or output or both) the analyst determines the total number of characters (number of messages × characters per message) entering and leaving that location during the peak period. He must then reduce the rate to characters per second, since most devices "rated speed" are expressed in that unit of time.

By using the number of characters entering (and leaving) each location, the analyst can determine the data transmission requirements. He will find that he can automatically eliminate many possibilities, for instance, those that exceed requirements (too fast) as well as those that will not be able to maintain the level of thruput (too slow).

TERMINAL LOCATION WORKSHEET

Date: _1/30/–_

Application: _Inventory Control_

Analyst: _a. allen_

Terminal No.	Location of Terminal	Transactions Entered/(Received)	Trans. No.	Type of Device	No. Msgs. (Peak Period)	No. Char. (Peak Period)	Cost of Unit (per month)	Comments
1	Alongside Receiving Clerk desk	1. Receipt of goods	I 0012		230/hr	40		
		2. Acknowledgment of receipt	O 0014		230/hr	40		
		3. Returns	I 0013		80 /hr	40		
		4. Acknowledgment of Returns	O 0015		80 /hr	40		

Figure 7.10

In the Receiving Department example, shown in Figures 7.8, 7.9, and 7.10, it was determined that the message volumes (shown in Figure 7.11) for all applications would be taking place during the peak period. With 3.85 (231.2/60) characters per second being entered into the system from this one location, high speed terminal devices operating in the 2000+ characters per second range are too fast. Intermediate speed devices in the 50- to 300-characters-per-second range are also higher than estimated needs. In this instance a low speed device is needed. The same reasoning applies to output messages. Since there appears little need for a machine intelligible document to be output by the computer and since the messages are variable in length, a typewriter would seem to be suitable for this location. Checking a specification manual, the analyst will find the rated speed that a typewriter can print messages sent from the computer to be approximately 14 characters per second. Typing messages *into* the system, of course, depends on the capability of the operator. A person with average typing skill can type between 2 to 5 characters per second. It appears, therefore, that two Input/Output typewriters are needed to serve the needs of the Receiving Department. Once the analyst has determined the number of characters per second going to and from each location, for all applications, he can concentrate on those devices operating at a speed that is within the range of the number of characters anticipated. To determine which type of device to use he will need answers to the following partial list of questions.

Inputs

1. Is it efficient to first prepare the input data off-line and then send it to the computer?

    (If yes, a card or paper tape reader may be the unit to use.)

2. Is hard copy of input messages required? (If the answer is no and a copy of output messages is also not required then a graphic display device may be useful.)

3. Do the input messages vary in length? (If yes, a typewriter, rather than a card reader, for inputting prepunched cards, can be used.)

Outputs

1. Does each output message contain a large number of characters *and* is hard copy required? (If the answer to the first part of the question is yes and the second no, then a graphic display can be used.)

CHARACTER VOLUMES WORKSHEET

Date: ___2/6/—___

Analyst: ___A. Allen___

Location: ___Receiving Department___

Type of Message	No. Msgs.	Per (unit of time)	No. Char. per msg.*	Total No. Char. (per min.)
A. Input (to the computer)				
1. Receipt of goods from outside sources.	230	Hour	40	$153.3^{(i)}$
2. Returns	80	Hour	40	53.0
3. Corrections, mis.	3	Hour	27	1.4**
4. Inquiries	40	Hour	40	26.7
5. Answer to inquiries	32	Day(8 hrs, 480 min.)	12	0.8
				231.2
B. Output (from the computer)				
1. Reserve quantity of items to be issued for a specification.	31	Hour	28	$14.5^{(ii)}$
2. Inquiry quantity on hand	3	Hour	12	0.6
3. Transfer orders	10	Day	36	0.8
4. Change to previously issued order	5	Day	65	0.7
				16.6

* Including Functional Characters

** Rounded Upward

i —— (230 × 40/60)

ii —— (31 × 28/60)

Figure 7.11

2. At some future time does the output message become an input into the system?

(If yes, a card or paper tape punch unit may be required.)

Once the analyst determines which type of terminal to be used he can enter in the Terminal Location Worksheet, the device he has selected (under heading TYPE OF DEVICE). Alongside is placed the approximate cost of the device and *terminal* control unit.

The list of selected devices should be reviewed to see if by varying the input or output media a greater efficiency, for the terminal operator(s) and/or the system flow, can be obtained. If an improvement can be made at a lower cost the type of terminal device should be modified on the Terminal Location Sheet. If the improvement results in a higher equipment cost a careful analysis of trade-offs must be made.

In generally it is considered advisable to keep the number of vendors supplying equipment to the real-time system to a minimum. Although there may be cheaper devices available, problems arising from dealing with many manufacturers can often outweigh any savings in equipment rental. Some of the difficulties encountered when dealing with more than one equipment manufacturer are the following:

(a) Different interface specifications—there are at present, no industry standards for the connections of equipment. Manufacturers often take different engineering approaches.

(b) Additional systems' analysis, programming, and engineering may be required, thus increasing problems, costs, and time required for implementation of the system.

(c) When an equipment failure takes place it is difficult to assign responsibility for the malfunction.

SPECIFY THE COMMUNICATION NETWORK

When specifying the communication network, the system analyst is answering the following question: While maintaining the response time requirements of the system, what is the most economical way of connecting the terminals to the computer? If the analyst uses a map to plot the location of each terminal he will see that there are many ways of connecting them to the main computer. Figure 7.12 shows four ways communication lines can connect three terminals to the computer. In a network of 15 terminal locations, the number of possible combinations in a 15-terminal system is 15! more than 75 billion different network configurations.

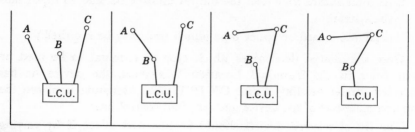

Figure 7.12

This question becomes more difficult to solve when one includes various tariffs and the fact that lines should be balanced (all lines carry approximately the same number of characters in any given period). Although there are techniques for manually developing a network, a more optimal solution, one with a lower line cost, can be developed with the use of a line loading computer program. (Also called Network Analysis Program.) A line loading program can supply information such as line utilization, response time; and specify actual network, and its cost along with the number and type of lines required. Besides supplying a network it is easy to develop a new network if changes to terminal specification are required. These programs are available from many of the common carriers and computer manufacturers.

DETERMINE THE TYPE AND NUMBER OF LINE CONTROL UNIT(S)

Once the number and type of lines has been determined, the specification of the Network Control Unit is a comparatively simple matter since most equipment manufacturers have only one or two units for a given range (number) of communication lines; for example, there is only one unit available from a given manufacturer for a system having 1 to 4 lines, and another unit for a system with 5 to 15 lines. For real-time systems with a limited number of lines, most manufacturers offer data exchanges. For larger systems, 40+ lines, multiplexors are available. A multiplexor is more advisable with larger systems because of more demanding control functions, higher message volumes, and larger communication core storage requirements. In those instances where the analyst has a choice between two smaller capacity units or one larger unit, it then becomes a question involving cost of equipment and reliability.

CONCLUSION

The steps involved in the specification of the terminal, line, and line control unit(s) consist of the following:

1. List all message types.
2. Determine the lengths of each message type.
3. Determine the number of input and output messages occurring during each location's peak period.
4. After reviewing available types of terminals, based on the volume and requirements at each location, select the type and number of units to be used at each of these sites.
5. Input the information developed in steps 1 through 4 above into a Network Analysis Program to determine the communication facilities needed by the system.
6. Review the terminal and network configuration to determine if adjustments can reduce line costs without adversely affecting the efficiency of the system.
7. Using the information outputted from the final running of the Network Analysis Program determine the type and number of Line Control Unit(s) required.

The specification of the communication equipment completes the hardware specification phase of the system study on an individual component basis. The system that has been designed must now be reviewed to ensure that, when all units are functioning together as an integrated system, thruput requirements can be maintained.

CHAPTER 8

Simulation

UP TO NOW WE HAVE CONSIDERED THE DESIGN PROBLEMS FOR EACH PART OF A REAL-TIME SYSTEM WITHOUT NECESSARILY CONSIDERING THE INTERACTIONS BETWEEN THESE COMPONENTS. IT IS NOW NECESSARY TO CONSIDER THE PROBLEMS INVOLVED WHEN THE COMPONENTS ARE WORKING TOGETHER IN A COMPLETE SYSTEM. MOST OF THESE DESIGN PROBLEMS ARE RELATED TO THE CENTRAL QUESTION: "DOES THE SYSTEM MEET THE THRUPUT AND RESPONSE TIME REQUIREMENTS?" THIS CHAPTER WILL DESCRIBE A VERY IMPORTANT TECHNIQUE FOR ANSWERING THIS QUESTION, THAT OF DIGITAL COMPUTER SIMULATION.

THE TIMING PROBLEM IN A REAL-TIME SYSTEM

Probably the most important aspect of any computer system is time—the time required to process a given set of transactions. Before timing complex equipment interactions, let us first review some basic timing concepts. Figure 8.1 is a flow chart of an extremely simple computer application. The time to perform each *element* of the application is indicated beside that element. The total time to complete the processing of one transaction is the sum of the element times—that is, $12 + 5 + 13 = 30$ ms. There is, associated with this time, a measure of system capability called system thruput. The thruput of the system designed to process this application, in transactions per minute, can be determined by

$$\text{thruput} = \frac{60,000 \text{ ms per min}}{\text{ms to process one transaction}} = \frac{60,000 \text{ ms}}{30 \text{ ms}} = 2000 \text{ transactions per min}$$

The preceding calculation assumes no process overlap.[1] If overlap were possible, with the computer that had been selected, the timing chart in Figure 8.2 indicates the savings that could be achieved. It would take 50 ms to process two transactions, or 25 ms per transaction.

---

[1] Process overlap is the ability of a computer to process a transaction at the same time an Input-Output operation is taking place.

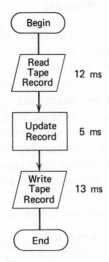

Figure 8.1. Simple timing problem.

Thruput of 2400 transactions per minute is determined by the same method of calculation used previously.

Note that this application has three significant attributes which make the task of determining thruput a simple one.

1. The flow of work is simple and direct.
2. The "element times" [2] are constants.
3. The input rate is under the control of the computer.

Not one of these features is present in real-time systems. For illustrative purposes, however, these three characteristics will be withdrawn one at a time to indicate their impact on real-time system timing problems.

[2] Element time, used throughout this chapter, is the time required by a computer to process or complete a section of a program.

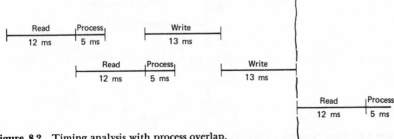

Figure 8.2. Timing analysis with process overlap.

MULTIPLE PATHS IN A PROGRAM

The first change in the example will be the inclusion of multiple paths. As shown in Figure 8.3, a decision is made in the middle of the program and either of two paths can be taken, depending on the decision's outcome. To determine processing time in this situation, it must be ascertained how often each path is followed. Suppose the decision is to be made on some characteristic of the input data.

The total process time for one transaction concerned with one record type is $12 + 5 + 3 + 13 = 33$ ms. For the other type, $12 + 5 + 13 = 30$ ms are required. If it is known in advance that 30 percent of the records will require 33 ms and 70 percent will require 30 ms, the average process time would be $33 \times 0.30 + 30 \times 0.70 = 9.90 + 21.00 = 30.9$ ms. The average number of records that could be processed each minute would be

$$\frac{60,000 \text{ ms per min}}{30.9 \text{ ms per record}} = 1941.4 \text{ transactions per min}$$

Note that in this example the process time is not represented by a single value. Rather, it is represented by a *probability distribution* which

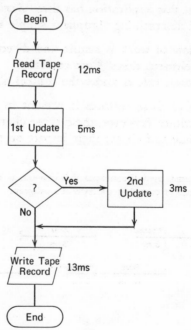

Figure 8.3. More complex timing problem.

lists each possible value of process time, together with the percentage, or probability, of its occurrence.

The concept of probability distribution is illustrated graphically in Figure 8.4. The possible values of the variable are indicated on the horizontal axis and the probability of occurrence of any value on the vertical axis. The average, or *mean*, processing time is determined by "weighting" each possible value by its probability and then adding the results. Probability distribution is an important tool in timing any system because most programs have many diverse paths to and from subroutines and Input-Output functions. In order to construct a distribution for any routine, an understanding of these probabilities is essential. In systems where the only source of variation is a completely definable set of paths, the average process time can be determined solely by means of computational effort.

In our example the paths were defined by the two types of records, but if the exact percentages of these records were unknown, the distribution (and therefore, the average process time) could not have been determined. This problem of not knowing the percentages associated with the multiple paths of a program occurs quite frequently in real-time systems. For example, the monitor or control program may have a very large number of paths, each one depending on the prevailing system conditions at a given time. It is usually extremely difficult to know in advance how often any set of conditions will occur, and more often than not, a reasonable guess will be required.

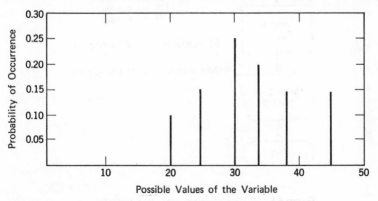

Figure 8.4. Probability distribution.

RANDOMNESS IN THE ELEMENT TIMES

The second source of variation which complicates program timing is the presence of randomness in the element times. The times for some blocks in the flow chart are not constants but must be represented by means of a probability distribution. Such randomness may be due to equipment characteristics and/or Input-Output considerations. One source of randomness would be variable length records in the input file, which would cause the read/write time to vary with the length of each record.

Another type of randomness in element times is caused by the manner in which the equipment operates. One such type of Input-Output equipment is the "random access device" (disk files, drums, etc.). To illustrate the factors which affect the access times to these devices, consider the diagram in Figure 8.5.

In order to perform an Input-Output operation on such a device, two separate functions must be performed. First, the access mechanism must be positioned onto the appropriate track in the file. The range of times for this "seek" function are given in Figure 8.5. The exact time in any particular case depends on the position of the mechanism before this operation and the track to which it must move. This is, in turn, a func-

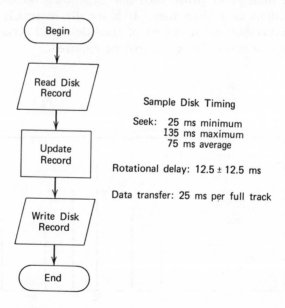

Figure 8.5. Timing problem with disk records.

tion of "file organization," that is, the manner in which records are distributed throughout the disk file unit. Using the simplest of file organization, as an example, if all the records are spread equally over all tracks, it is possible to calculate the "seek time distribution" based on the fact that the access mechanism will, at a given time, just as likely be on one track as on any other. The techniques of basic probability theory have, in fact, been used to do this. The resulting distribution can be used to determine an "Average Seek Time," which is indicated in the diagram as 75 ms.

The second function performed in any Input-Output operation is the actual transmission of data (Read, Write). The time required for a transmission is composed of two parts: (a) *rotational delay*, the time required for the rotation of the disk to bring the start of the desired record exactly into position under the read/write head of the access mechanism; and (b) *the data transfer*, the actual read or write time. If the time for a complete revolution is 25 ms, we can specify the distribution of rotational delay time as 12.5 ± 12.5 ms—that is, any value between 0 and 25 ms. The average rotational delay is 12.5 ms. The reason for this is that the start of the desired record can be any place on the track, relative to the position of the access mechanism when it reaches the track. Data transfer times on random access devices range from 90,000 to 300,000 characters per second. To transfer a record occupying an entire track, the following times would apply, using 25 ms per revolution:

rotational delay	12.5 ± 12.5 ms,
data transfer	25 ms,
Total	37.5 ± 12.5 ms.

We see then that the Input-Output time distributions for any system are dependent on at least three factors: (1) the characteristics of the equipment (data transfer time, rotational delays, access motion time); (2) file organization (random, sequential, etc); and (3) record lengths.

RANDOM ARRIVAL RATES

The one remaining feature of our basic example which is to be withdrawn is that concerning the "controlled input rate." For most commercial real-time systems, the exact times at which input messages will enter the system are not completely known, nor can they be controlled. These "arrival rates" can only be estimated by means of probability distributions. The interaction of all three of these factors (random arrival times, multiple processing paths, and random element times) is usually just enough to cause a complete breakdown in purely analytical timing methods.

Ordinarily, most batch applications with complex flows, random access devices, variable length tape records, etc., can still be represented as "static" systems with one transaction being handled at a time. This is not so with real-time systems, because the introduction of random arrival times makes the system truly "dynamic." A timing analysis cannot examine one transaction at a time, because the system does not operate that way. (Even if the central computer only considers one message at a time, the entire system—lines, terminals, storage devices and multiplexor(s)—is operating with an "unpredictable" random stream of messages.) Mathematicians formally classify these systems as "queuing systems," to indicate that messages form waiting lines behind the various facilities (computer, terminal, etc.,) and usually move from one waiting line to another in random fashion.

Whenever random arrivals are present in a system, a non-analytic technique usually must be employed. Here a page can be taken from the physical sciences. Early in the development of these disciplines, it was realized that mathematical formulations would not suffice to explain the particular systems being studied. Experiments had to be performed to corroborate or disprove particular hypotheses and contribute to a better understanding of the system. This is exactly what must be done in the discipline of designing real-time systems. The experimental technique employed for this purpose is simulation.

SIMULATION

The term simulation can be used to describe a variety of techniques. One must, therefore, be explicit in defining its usage in the area of real-time systems. As has already been indicated, simulation is an experimental technique and is concerned with studying a sample of the whole environment. This point must not be ignored. As an experiment, simulation must study a sample of "typical" messages that enter the system. Inferences about system behavior at all times must be drawn from the results of this study.

Historically, there have been two types of experimentation in the physical sciences. The first involves studying the actual physical system in a limited fashion. The second involves building a "model" of the system for use in a laboratory environment. The latter method has usually been employed for studying "proposed" systems, those which are in their design phase, because there is no "actual" system to study.

Real-time system simulation lies in this category. Whereas traditional experimental models are usually simplified *physical* versions of actual systems, real-time simulation models are *logical* versions of their parent systems. When these logical models are too complex to be examined manually, they are usually analyzed on a digital computer. Some exact methods for representing real-time systems with logical models will be examined in the next few sections.

BUILDING THE LOGICAL MODEL

The simulation of a real-time system has three identifying characteristics:

1. It is a method for predicting system behavior.
2. It is an experiment which examines a sample from the whole environment.
3. It utilizes a logical model on a digital computer.

In a typical real-time system, messages "arrive" from remote terminals, are received by the multiplexor, and proceed to the computer, encountering delays at various points in the flow. The major sources of variability in such a system are as follows:

1. The arrival rates are random variables that may differ from terminal to terminal.
2. Data transmission times are functions of the various message lengths.
3. The time a message is queued in the multiplexor at any given time varies with the load on the system.
4. Control program execution time varies with the number and type of messages currently in the computer.
5. The processing "branch" to be taken in the computer depends on the input message type.[3]
6. Random access times are functions of the file organization for any given record type.

These sources of variation interact in various ways to produce delays at key points in the flow. It can easily be seen that no simple analysis could determine the processing capability of such a system. The various factors in the system must be logically represented to a specially designed

---

[3] The distribution of message types at each terminal can usually be determined from knowledge of the application. These distributions must be "pooled" to get a distribution within the computer.

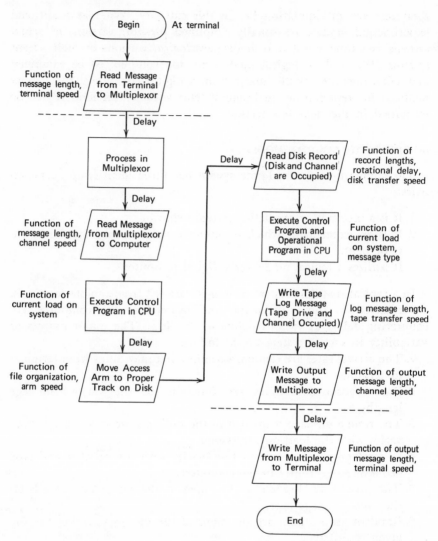

Figure 8.6. Consolidated flow in real-time system. (Blocks between dashed lines represent processing at the central computer only.)

computer program, a simulator, which in turn can "experiment" with this logical representation.

Suppose the problem is temporarily simplified, and the analyst is only interested in determining the maximum thruput attainable in the central computer system, which includes the multiplexor. The flow can then be shown in a "consolidated" form (as in Figure 8.6), starting at the terminal. Next to each element in this flow are the factors which determine each element time.

To represent such a flow logically to a simulator, it is necessary to indicate the routing for each message type and to specify the exact physical parts of the system that are to be used. In addition, all variables pertaining to the flow must be described, by distributions if necessary.

1. Message type distribution (consolidated).
2. Input message length distribution (for each type).
3. Tape log message length distribution (for each type).
4. Output message length distribution (for each type).
5. Data transmission rates (for each I-O device).
6. Seek time distribution (for each type, if necessary).
7. Disk file record length distribution (for each type).
8. Control program time distribution.
9. Operational program time distribution (for each type).

AN IMPORTANT SIMULATION LANGUAGE

There are many ways by which the major characteristics of a real-time system can be specified to a digital computer for purposes of performing a simulation. This section will describe just one method for supplying this information. The method is a well known simulation language developed several years ago at IBM called the General Purpose Simulation System (GPSS).

The GPSS language makes it possible to describe a real-time system in very concise terms with only a fraction of the detail that would be needed in a lower level language, such as assembly language or even some compiler languages. The general principle of the GPSS language is that, in most "particle-flow" systems—such as computers processing data records, cars passing through toll booths, or orders being routed through a job shop—there are many common features. First, there are the "particles" themselves, which GPSS calls "transactions." Next, there are various types of physical units which must be accessed by the transaction. Whenever access cannot be obtained immediately, transactions must wait, and the set of transactions waiting for access to a physical unit becomes a waiting line or a "queue." GPSS takes advantage of these common features by providing a block diagramming technique and a set of rules for using its various types of blocks.

The best way to demonstrate the GPSS approach is to use a physical example. Consider just one part of the flow in Figure 8.6, that of

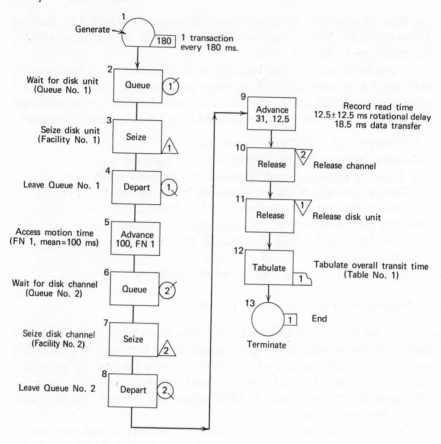

Figure 8.7. GPSS block diagram of disk reading.

accessing the disk unit and the disk channel in order to read a record into core. Figure 8.7 shows a GPSS block diagram for this problem. Each of these blocks will be explained in detail.

Block 1 generates the transaction according to a specified arrival interval (one every 180 ms). Block 2 directs the simulator program to enter the transaction in Queue No. 1. The transaction will remain in this queue until Facility No. 1 (the disk unit) is available. Block 3 indicates that the transaction is attempting to access the disk unit. So long as this unit is not available, the transaction is "held up" in Block 2. If the disk unit becomes available, the transaction can pass through Block 3 and into Block 4, which directs the simulator to record that the transaction is no longer in Queue No. 1.

Block 5 specifies the time for which the disk unit must be occupied by the transaction in order to position its access mechanism over the proper disk track. This time is given by Function No. 1 (FN1), which is a probability distribution with a mean time of 100 ms. The simulator program must record this occupation time for Facility No. 1. Next, the transaction enters Queue No. 2, which represents the delay the transaction encounters in trying to access the disk channel (Facility No. 2). When access is obtained, the transaction passes through Blocks 6, 7, and 8 in the same manner as before.

Block 9 specifies the time for which the disk unit and the disk channel are used in reading the given data record. This time is 31 ± 12.5 ms, which indicates that any time between 18 ms and 44 ms is possible and that each time has an equal probability of occurrence. This time really has two parts: first, rotational delay, based on 25 ms for one revolution of the disk, so that any time between 0 and 25 ms might be required to position the access mechanism over the point where the record begins on the track; second, the time to transfer the data in the record, which depends on record length and disk speed.

Although the above example is quite simple, it does show the basic features of the GPSS language. Of course, most actual simulation problems are extremely complex, which can be surmised by recalling that this example represents only one small part of the overall flow in Figure 8.7. However, GPSS can handle these complexities quite easily. Among the major features not shown in the examples are:

1. The ability to direct the flow into several different paths, depending on certain conditions.
2. The ability to show many paths being executed simultaneously. For example, it can represent a transaction trying to read two records from different disk channels at the same time.
3. The ability to store special information about individual transactions by means of "transaction parameters."
4. The ability to maintain different priority levels and priority disciplines for transactions competing for a given facility.
5. The ability to represent physical units which may be accessed simultaneously by more than one transaction up to a specified maximum. These units are called "storages," instead of "facilities" which may be accessed by one transaction at a time. An example of a "storage" would be computer core storage, which can contain more than one message but has a definite limit.
6. The ability to tabulate almost any statistic relating to the simulation. These include transit times, queue lengths, facility and storage

utilizations, and the values of any transaction parameters. These statistics will be discussed more extensively below.

As mentioned earlier, GPSS is only one method for constructing a simulation model. Other languages have been and are being developed. Probably the most well known of these is SIMSCRIPT, which is described in reference (2). This language is quite general, as is GPSS. Other approaches have concentrated on the particular types of systems being studied; for example, several people have written simulators for computing systems. The advantage of these approaches is that the input can be supplied in highly descriptive language which is more problem oriented. For example, transactions can be called "messages," or facilities can be referred to by their real names ("CPU," "disk," "channel," etc.). Whatever type of language is employed, all the simulators follow the same general principles.

Operating with GPSS

As shown in the block diagram of Figure 8.7, each block type in GPSS has a unique shape for the purpose of standardization, and although it is quite useful to follow these standards, the simulator program doesn't depend on them. Instead, for each block in the diagram a card containing the block type identification (SEIZE, ADVANCE, etc.) and the other information required to describe the block must be punched; for example, in a QUEUE block the Queue Number must be included; and in an ADVANCE block the time factors must be included.

In addition to the cards for the various blocks in the model, certain other definition cards are required. These include cards to specify capacities of any storages in the model, cards to define the various tables, and cards to specify any special computations to be made.

Once the whole simulation model is coded, it is supplied as input to a simulator program. Many computer manufacturers, in addition to IBM, now provide a GPSS package to their users. The exact methods for coding both the block cards and the definition cards are well documented in the manuals provided by these manufacturers.

The basic operation of a simulator program consists of generating transactions and keeping track of the facilities and storages being accessed by these transactions. In addition, the program must maintain a "clock" to record the passage of time and to determine what activities are to take place at various times. To allow for probability and randomness, which is the basic reason for using simulation, the program must also have a "random number generator." This generator actually samples one value from a given distribution each time the distribution is encountered. By running the simulator program long enough, it is hoped that each distribution will be sampled often enough to reflect all points on the distribution. Of course, this question about the validity of the sampling procedure is very complex and will be treated more thoroughly in a later section.

It is not possible in this type of presentation to describe the exact procedures employed in a simulator program. For those who wish to study these procedures, a detailed explanation has been provided in Appendix A. This appendix is recommended for anyone who wishes to obtain more than a cursory understanding of simulation techniques.

SIMULATION OUTPUT AND ITS USE

The objective of a simulation is to produce an estimate of a given system's performance. There are several output possibilities implied by the procedures shown in the previous sections. Each of these will be discussed here.

The easiest, and probably the most important, statistic to determine is the estimate of *system thruput*. This can be obtained by using an arbitrarily large arrival rate and recording the number of transactions which were processed during the period of the simulation run. If 6600 were processed during a 10-minute run, then the estimate of thruput is 660 per minute. This statistic is usually very valuable in determining whether a proposed design is in the neighborhood of a correct solution. For example, if the application is expected to have an input of 1000 transactions a minute during its peak period, the thruput estimate of 660 would immediately indicate a deficiency in the system design. It should be pointed out, however, that, if the thruput estimate is in the neighborhood of the application requirement, we are still not assured that the system is adequate. This point will be brought into focus when discussing other types of output reports.

Another useful statistic is the *average utilization* of a facility. This can be determined for as many facilities as desired. Utilization is a measure of a facility's busy time versus over-all run time. The number of time units in which the facility is busy is accumulated during any interval. At the end this cumulative busy time is divided by total run time to get average utilization. The major use of this statistic is to locate any "bottleneck" facilities which would correspond, of course, to weak points in the system.

In the first set of runs for a simulation model, an infinite arrival rate at the computing center is usually assumed. This assumption can prove very valuable in conjunction with the statistics for thruput and average utilization. If the thruput estimate is less than required, the average utilization can point out the cause, or causes, of the trouble. Under the input assumption, any facility with an average utilization near 100 percent is a bottleneck. Even if the thruput is greater than required, a 100 percent utilized facility will indicate the barrier to be overcome if the system should ever have to be expanded. This "infinite arrival rate" assumption is, therefore, a good first attempt at evaluating the system.

If system thruput is greater than required, the proposed design is in the right neighborhood of a solution—that is, the system could process all transactions without developing interminable delays or infinite queues. However, most systems usually have more stringent performance requirements; for example, in an airlines reservation system, certain transaction types may not be permitted to take longer than a specified amount of time. This would be especially true with inquiry messages. It becomes necessary, then, to estimate system behavior in more detail. First the required system input rate can be used as the mean arrival rate in the simulation model. Then, based on the conditions of the particular application, a probability distribution can be applied to this mean arrival rate. The most common distribution to be employed is the Poisson distribution. This type of distribution has the property that the number of arrivals during any interval is completely independent of the number in any previous interval. This "random" property usually corresponds to a worst case, thus permitting the simulator to generate wide variations from the mean. In general, this selection of an arrival distribution should be made with the help of a statistician.

In the second set of simulation runs, the major statistic to be obtained is an estimate of the transit time distribution for all transaction types. Transit time is the total time spent by a transaction in the system, from its generation until its removal. Therefore, the time spent by each transaction can be recorded as it terminates. Transaction times can then be segregated into specified intervals, and at the end of the run, the *frequency distribution* of transit time can be listed. If the number of transactions in each interval is divided by the total number of transactions, the result is a *probability distribution* which indicates the chances of the transit time being in a particular interval. In addition, the mean and standard deviation of this distribution can be computed. The upper intervals of this distribution can be examined to determine the chances (if any) of a transit time exceeding a specified maximum, as per the airlines reservation sample.

Three other types of output may also be significant in the second set of runs. The first is *average utilization,* which can again indicate the relative importance of various facilities and also whether any facilities are dangerously near the 100 percent mark. The second is the *waiting time distribution* at each facility, which can be obtained in the same manner as transit time distribution and is another measure of the facility's importance. The third is a *queue length distribution,* which indicates the number of transactions waiting at a given facility. This also indicates a facility's significance, but more important, it can provide a good idea of the core storage requirements in the system, since items which wait must have a location in which to wait. The queue length distribution can be obtained by recording the number of transactions waiting for a facility at the end of each of several fixed time intervals; for example, every five seconds. At the end of the run, the queue lengths can be segregated and listed in a distribution form.

If the simulation model was constructed via the GPSS language, some of the statistics mentioned here would be generated automatically, namely the average facility and storage utilizations and the average queue lengths. Other key system variables are maintained by the program, and the other types of reports desired can be specified in the table definition cards at the beginning of the run.

EXTENDING THE LOGICAL SIMULATION MODEL

After the performance of the computing center has been thoroughly studied, it is usually necessary to extend the model to include the multiplexor, the communication lines, and the terminals. The major reason for studying the computer first is to guarantee a sufficient capacity at the center of the system. Once this can be assured, the proposed communication system design can be evaluated. Again there is a two-fold requirement:

1. The system must be able to process all inputs without causing interminable delays, and
2. The transactions must meet some response time specifications.

The lines, terminals, and multiplexor should be modeled in the same manner as the computing center, indicating facilities, processing time (if it is significant), and the particular polling discipline used. This will be added to the original model in place of the "combined arrival rate" that was originally used. The arrivals will now take place at individual terminals according to some specified distribution (usually Poisson). The same types of statistics, especially transit times, can be obtained, and these will provide an evaluaton of the over-all system.

TECHNIQUES IN LIEU OF SIMULATION

There are other methods, particularly probability and queuing theory, which can be employed for evaluating a system's performance. At present, none of these other technques is as applicable as simulation. There may, however, be certain situations in which the use of probability and queuing theory, together with some algebra, can help to answer the same questions as simulation. These situations are not common, especially with the large scale systems being designed today. However, the systems designer should be aware of the applicability of approaches other than simulation. The usual circumstances of such a special case are as follows:

1. The first condition is a "one at a time" system, that is there is no multiprogramming. Messages are stored either in the multiplexor or in the computer's core storage itself, but only one transaction is processed at a time through its operational program, including all its Input-Output operations.
2. The second condition is a Poisson arrival distribution—an assumption which, as pointed out earlier, is common today.
3. A third, and very important condition, is exclusive interest in determining the average transit time per transaction, without considering the differences in transaction types or the whole distribution of transit times.

These conditions have been deliberately chosen for illustrative purposes, but I have been confronted with this set of circumstances in various design problems. (It usually takes the form of a question, "If we had a very simple system with no multiprogramming, could the desired thruput be achieved"? The answer is usually "no," but it's worth the effort to analyze the system using these techniques.)

This estimating problem can be approached by first determining the *mean* processing time per transaction in the system. Algebraic techniques can be used for this, by examining all the possible paths in the program and the element times for each subroutine and I-O operation, including disk, tape, and communications with the terminal. Next, the *variance* of process time can be determined. This is a measure of the variability in the process time distribution and is computed by taking the average value of the squared differences between the mean and each possible value of the process time.

Once the mean and variance of the process time distribution are known, some useful formulas from queuing theory can be applied to solve for

(a) the average utilization of the computer system, or the percent of time the system is processing messages rather than waiting for messages to arrive.

(b) the average waiting time for a message before being processed by the computer,

(c) the average transit time for a message, including waiting and processing,

(d) the average number of messages waiting to be processed,

(e) the average number of messages in the system, including waiting and processing.

The following formulas are given without proof:*

(a) $U =$ average utilization

$U = ma$

where $a =$ average arrival rate of messages to the computer
(for example, 2 messages per second)
$m =$ average (mean) process time in the computer
(for example, 400 ms per message)

(b) $W =$ average waiting time

$$W = \frac{mU}{2(1-U)} [1 + V/m^2]$$

where $V =$ variance of process time in the computer

(c) $T =$ average transit time

$$T = W + m$$

(d) $N =$ average number of messages waiting

$$N = Wa$$

(e) $W =$ average number of messages in the system

$$W = Ta$$

If the above conditions were met in a system, this approach would in fact be better than simulation, because this is an analytic method capable

* These formulas can be found in several texts and papers on queuing theory. Reference (4) was used here.

of determining the exact value of mean transit time. Simulation is an experiment, and any results constitute a sample estimate of the actual mean transit time. The longer the simulation run, the more accurate the estimate, but it is still an estimate.

This example does not exhaust the possibilities for applying queuing theory in place of simulation. There has been considerable development in the general area of queuing theory, and more can be expected. Some of this work is particularly applicable to real-time system evaluation. Usually, the formulas developed in such research can be used to obtain rough estimates of either the total performance of a system, or of a particular section of the system, prior to building the simulation model. This provides the designer with a preliminary insight to the system and a better knowledge of the kind of information he will need from the simulation.

PITFALLS IN USING SIMULATION

Nothing is perfect. Bad simulations, however, have their special brand of imperfection—errors which are rarely discovered until too late. There are two sources of error in simulation, each of them extremely difficult to detect unless the proper precautions are taken.

The first source of error is "bad logic"—that is, an inaccurate representation of the system to the simulation program. Unlike most logical models which are run on a computer, a simulation model cannot be tested and debugged, except in a very superficial way, because there are no "test data" available for comparing the simulation results. When an *existing* system is being simulated, the model is verified by comparing its results with the actual performance of the system. No such system exists in the design stage. The possibilities are enormous for (1) misunderstanding the many details of a proposed design, or (2) inaccurately translating the design features into a set of logical rules for the simulator to follow. The only way that such errors can be avoided is by "desk checking"—that is, by reviewing the model several times, preferably by more than one person. Incidentally, this "problem" can be a blessing in disguise, as it forces the system designer to review carefully all his assumptions and their implications. It would be a highly unusual situation if no revisions in the design were brought about as a result of subjecting the assumptions to this kind of scrutiny.

The second source of error is improper evaluation of the simulation results. *Simulation is an experiment.* No matter how loudly one proclaims the results, it does not change this fact. As an experiment, it is subject to what statiticians call "sampling error." Every result of a simulation run, whether it is thruput, utilization, or the number of transit times lying in a given interval, has an associated "confidence interval." Statisticians often determine 95 percent confidence limits about any particular value. For example, if the value of system thruput in a simulation run was 500 transactions per minute, the statistician might set up an interval between 480 and 520 and state that we can be 95 percent certain that the true system thruput lies in this range. The factors which determine the confidence interval are the variability of the data and the length of the run. The smaller the variability or the longer the run, the shorter the confidence interval.

In evaluating simulation results, the aid of a professional statistician is usually required. If the results are so indicative of a proposed system's capability to do the job that they do not even require statistical analysis, it is quite likely that the system has been "overdesigned." Most of the time, this will not be the case. A good statitsical analysis should be considered an absolute necessity. In fact, the time to make first contact with the statistician is *before* building the model. He can provide many useful ideas for designing the simulation experiment (length of run, distributions to be used, etc.). In some cases, the statistician may even recommend an alternative approach, such as queuing theory.

To summarize the pitfalls in simulation, the following procedure is recommended to ensure a good simulation with minimum error:

1. As soon as a proposed design is complete and ready for analysis, consult with a statistician. At best, he may provide an analytic technique. He can give valuable advice in designing the experiment if simulation is necessary.
2. Build the logical model, with constant review of the design assumptions and the model's representation of these assumptions.
3. Run the logical model on the simulator.
4. Analyze the simulation results, consulting with a statistician to determine confidence limits on the output variables.

ADVANCED APPLICATION OF THE MODEL

The simulation of a real-time system can be an expensive project, both in terms of computer hours and man-hours of model development. In a well-planned system study, however, this initial expense will be recovered through extensive use of the simulation model to study a variety of problems.

In most systems design problems, the situation is never quite so simple that there is only one design that has to be evaluated. Systems design usually involves the consideration of alternatives, and here is where simulation can have tremendous payoff. Without a simulation model, it would be extremely difficult to study more than a few alternatives in a particular system. However, a well-constructed model can usually be changed with only a little effort to reflect any alternative design consideration. This makes it possible to consider a lot more of these alternatives, and the result should be a more carefully designed system.

The possibilities for such design alternatives are quite numerous. A common alternative is duplexing, that is providing a second physical unit in certain parts of the system. Duplexing may involve an extra disk drive or an extra data channel. In some cases, it could involve an entire duplicate computer system. Sometimes, duplexing may be required solely because of reliability considerations, in order to decrease the system's expected down time. If this is the case, the simulation model can be used to predict how much "extra" performance will be obtained with this additional hardware if it is kept on line, at least during peak periods.

At the other extreme, the analyst might be interested in studying the system's performance if some of the terminals are removed, or if one fewer disk unit is employed. Does the performance degrade significantly? For example, if the average utilization of a terminal is 25 percent, perhaps some of that terminal's business could be transferred to another nearby terminal without affecting the over-all system performance.

There is no reason why the simulation effort need be confined to the design phase. Many problems arise during implementation which require changes to the system. Usually, decisions have to be made very quickly, and the simulation model can be very useful in evaluating these changes. In fact, a good case might be made for building a simulation model for use during implementation even if it were not used during the design phase. Of course, implementation also provides an opportunity to update the simulation model as more exact information about the system becomes available, and this opportunity shouldn't be ignored. The model should become more accurate as time passes, so that problems that arise at the eleventh hour can be studied and resolved with more confidence in the simulation results.

CONCLUSION

Simulation is an extremely powerful tool for studying the behavior of a real-time system. It must be used very carefully, however, and its results must be judged with the same kind of scientific rigor that is used in evaluating any kind of experimental studies. Under these circumstances, the benefits that can be obtained from a simulation model are more than adequate to pay for the cost involved.

As real-time systems become more commonplace, more emphasis will be placed on efficient systems design. In this type of environment, the more successful designers will probably be those who apply the most powerful techniques in building and evaluating their systems.

Digital computer simulation is the most powerful and advanced technique available today, and it will probably remain so for the next several years.

REFERENCES

1. IBM, "General Purpose Simulation System/360—Introductory User's Manual," IBM Form No. H20-0304.
2. Kiviat, P. J., R. Villanueva, and H. M. Markowitz, *The SIMSCRIPT II Programming Language,* Prentice-Hall, 1969.
3. Association for Computing Machinery, "Digest of the Second Conference on Applications of Simulation," 1968.
4. "Resume of Useful Formulas in Queuing Theory," Operations Research Volume 5 Number 2 (April 1957) pages 161-200.

CHAPTER 9

Completing The System Study

ALTHOUGH THE SYSTEM DESIGN EFFORT IS NEARLY COMPLETED, THERE ARE
DECISIONS THAT MUST STILL BE MADE CONCERNING THE FINAL CONFIGURATION
AS WELL AS FALLBACK AND RECOVERY PROCEDURES. THIS CHAPTER REVIEWS
THESE AREAS AS WELL AS PREPARATIONS OF THE FINAL STUDY REPORT.

Completion of the analysis of the thruput of the total system will
enable the study-team manager to determine

(a) If the system thruput has met systems requirements, and

(b) the utilization of each of the components.

If the results of this analysis show that the system has not met thruput
requirements, then one or more parts of the system will have to be
redesigned. Redesign can consist of:

1. increasing the amount of core storage so more transactions can enter
   computer memory;
2. reducing delays caused by transactions waiting for records by
   either
   (a) increasing the number of channels,
   (b) using a faster random access device for high activity records/
       programs, and/or
   (c) redistributing auxiliary storage units and/or the location of
       the data records so that each channel has the same percentage
       of utilization;
3. increasing the number of lines and/or the number of terminals,
   thus reducing the queues forming at the terminals;
4. reviewing with the steering committee the possibility of either
   increasing turn around time or processing only high priority messages during abnormal peak periods;
5. increasing the speed of the computer(s), thus reducing the utilization of a process-bound system.

The techniques available for improving system thruput can be seen
from the simulation results of the following configurations.

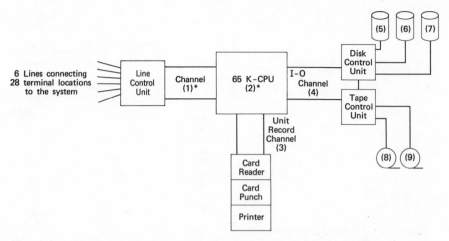

Figure 9.1. The first configuration (asterisk indicates the facility assignment number).

The first configuration simulated, shown in Figure 9.1, used an infinite transaction arrival rate. The results are shown in Table 9.1.

TABLE 9.1

Facility Number	Facility Assignment	Average Utilization	Average Queue Length	Maximum Queue Length
1	Terminal channel	(not included in first simulation)		
2	CPU	0.54 (54%)[1]	5	11
3	Unit record channel	0.73 (73%)	0	1
4	I-O channel	1.00	7	22
5	Disk no. 1	0.86	3	7
6	Disk no. 2	0.04	0	1
7	Disk no. 3	0.10	0	2
8	Tape no. 1	0.11	0	2
9	Tape no. 2	0.23	0	4

With this configuration the I-O channel was the component with the highest utilization. As the thruput did not meet system requirements, changes had to be made. Starting with the facility with the highest utilization—the I-O channel, a choice had to be made to specify either faster I-O devices or another channel. Since an additional channel was cheaper, the configuration was modified as shown in Figure 9.2.

[1] Average utilization is the percentage of total time that a component is unavailable (busy).

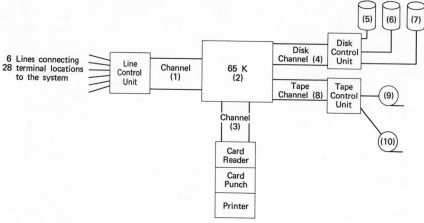

Figure 9.2. The second configuration.

The statistical information from the model simulating the new configuration is shown in Table 9.2.

TABLE 9.2

Facility Number	Facility Assignment	Average Utilization	Average Queue Length	Maximum Queue Length
1	Terminal channel	(not included in this simulation)		
2	CPU	0.63 (63%)	4	8
3	Unit record channel	0.72 (72%)	0	2
4	Disk channel	0.87	4	7
5	Disk no. 1	0.94	5	11
6	Disk no. 2	0.16	0	2
7	Disk no. 3	0.33	0	4
8	Tape channel	0.52	1	3
9	Tape no. 1	0.12	0	1
10	Tape no. 2	0.27	0	2

The thruput increased to 2.3 transactions per minute, placing it now in the "neighborhood" of the thruput specified by management. The system appeared not to be balanced—that is, one in which the average utilization of each of the components is approximately the same. The utilization of the disk channel was 87 percent, compared with 52 percent tape channel usage. There was also a wide variation of utilization of the disk drives 1, 2, and 3; 94, 16, and 33 percent, respectively. To reduce the queue length (wait time) for these facilities, the following changes were made:

1. The customer file was shifted to Disk Drive 2. Prior to this half of the customer file was on Drive 1 and the remainder on Drive 2.
2. The overflow area for the customer file was transferred entirely to Drive 1. Although this would increase the time required to obtain a customer record stored in the overflow area, it was decided that resequencing the customer file more often than originally intended would compensate for the increased record access time.
3. Transfer of the low usage error routines from Disk 2 to Disk 1. Modifying the model to reflect these changes increased the thruput to 2.9 transactions per minute and reduced the utilization and wait time (queue length) to that shown in Table 9.3.

TABLE 9.3

Facility	Average Utilization	Queue Length Average	Queue Length Maximum
Disk channel	0.84	2	5
Disk no. 1	0.81	2	6
Disk no. 2	0.46	1	4
Disk no. 3	0.44	0	3
Tape channel	0.50	1	3
Tape no. 1	0.12	0	1
Tape no. 2	0.25	0	2

Although it appeared possible to improve the balance of the system, additional changes were not run as a separate simulation run but were included with the expanded simulation model which included the lines and terminals. Even if the queue length could not be further reduced it was decided by the study-team manager that pending the results of the simulation of the entire system, a satisfactory system had been designed.

The critical component(s) are those with the highest utilization. Once the critical element has been identified, rearrangements of the system can be made. Techniques for improving thruput can be summarized as follows:

CRITICAL COMPONENT	POSSIBLE SYSTEM MODIFICATION
1. Terminals	a. Add more and/or faster (higher speed) units. b. If there is not an even distribution of line utilizations—transfer terminals to lines with lower utilizations.
2. Lines	a. Add more lines. b. Redistribute terminals changing line assignments to lines with lowest utilizations.
3. Line control unit	a. If only one L.C.U., add another. b. If two or more L.C.U.s, redistribute L.C.U.s line assignments.
4. L.C.U. channel	a. Add more L.C.U. channels. b. If unequal utilization of two or more L.C.U. channels, redistribute line assignments.
5. Unit record channel	a. Add unit record channel (s).
6. Central processor unit	a. Increase the speed of the central processor. b. Increase amount of core storage. c. Transfer operational programs from permanent core residence to auxiliary storage.
7. Auxiliary storage unit channels	a. Redistribute operational programs and data files among the disk units. b. Reassign drives among the channel(s). c. Increase the number of channels.

Simulation of the entire system will continue until a configuration which can maintain thruput requirements has been developed. Once the system has been made final the analysis can move on to the other areas which still have to be completed. They consist of

(a) determining the savings/costs of the new system,

(b) specifying alternate procedures of processing during periods of system unavailability,

(c) developing the implementation schedule, and

(d) presenting the system to management.

DETERMINING THE SAVINGS/COSTS OF THE NEW SYSTEM

SAVINGS

Vital to management are the savings that will accrue once the new system is running. These savings consist of dollar savings (displacable costs) and improved efficiencies. Displacable costs are those savings which will take place due to the elimination, reduction, or improvement of those functions which are a part of present data processing costs. There are three major areas in which savings can take place.

(a) *People:* The decreased number of personnel required for processing information is an important saving of a new system. The salaries of the people that are no longer needed should be ascertained. Included should be: (a) the amount of fringe benefits and other overhead costs; (b) the savings in salary costs whenever operating personnel do not have to be as highly skilled; (c) overtime that will no longer be required.

(b) *Equipment:* Equipment that will not be replaced since it will be obsolete with the new system is one source of savings. If the present items are sold the income should be considered as savings of the new system. Included are typewriters, file cabinets, bookkeeping machines, cardex files, and the like.

(c) *Forms:* The money spent annually on forms is considerable. The new system will reduce the type and number of forms required.

(d) *Miscellaneous:* In addition to these items there are savings which vary from business to business. Savings in floor space, telegrams, and long distance phone calls to expedite orders and postage are just a few.

The second type of savings, improved efficiencies, are intangible in nature and will not accrue until after the real-time system has become fully operational. It is difficult to obtain accurate dollar estimates for these types of savings. Items in this category are

(a) reduced obsolescence,
(b) increased turnover of inventory,
(c) interest saved from reduction of cash reserves,
(d) better utilization of capital equipment,
(e) availability of more up-to-date information,
(f) better control of decentralized operations, and
(g) rental of unutilized computer time.

COSTS

Counteracting these savings are the initial nonrecurring and running costs of installing and operating a new system. Initial one-time expenses are

    (a) preparing the computer room and the terminal locations,[2]
    (b) programming and testing, and
    (c) purchase of new equipment.

The running costs of the new system include

    (a) rental of the equipment;
    (b) salaries of the additional maintenance and systems programmers, computer operators, and supervisory staff;[3]
    (c) forms and paper;
    (d) additional overhead; and
    (e) miscellaneous items such as electricity and telephone.

These costs and savings can be summarized on a form similar to the one shown in Figure 9.3. On the bottom of the sheet are the net savings/increased costs (total savings minus all costs). Supplementing the summary sheet should be information as to how the amount attributed to each item was developed. The savings estimated should be conservative, the costs optimistic; thus allowing for unitemized additional unexpected costs.

SPECIFYING ALTERNATE PROCEDURES FOR PROCESSING DURING PERIODS OF SYSTEM UNAVAILABILITY

Since batch type computer systems are not directly linked to the immediate data processing needs of a company, when an equipment malfunction occurs processing stops. When the component is repaired, processing is restarted either from the beginning of the run or from the last checkpoint. In these types of systems there already exists a delay between the occurrence of the event and the results obtained from the computer. An equipment malfunction does not therefore introduce a delay—it only increases its duration.

The input transactions of a real-time system, however, are not under the control of the central processing unit(s). Since real-time systems are

---

[2] Many organizations amortize these costs over an extended period.

[3] The salaries of analysts and programmers adding new applications to the system once it is installed, should be costed against the individual applications.

Date: 5/14/____
Prepared by: A. Allen
Approved by: B. Johnson

Item	Amount (Per Year)	
A. Personnel	$120,000	
Overtime	5,000	
Capital Equipment	22,000	
Forms	6,000	
Misc.: Floor space	4,000	
Reduction of general overhead	30,000	$187,000
B. Intangible Savings		
+(Rental Income of Computer Time)		
Reduction Inventory–Obsolescence	20,000	
Cash reserves	–	
Bad debts	–	
Quicker payments	7,000	27,000
Total Savings		$214,000
C. One time costs: implementation (Costs amortized over 5 years)		60,000
D. Running Costs		
Rental of equipment	150,000	
Maintenance and systems programming	26,000	
Forms	2,000	
Electricity	8,000	
Additional computer operators	15,000	
Overhead	10,000	
Misc.	10,000	221,000
Total Costs		281,000
TOTAL		–$ 67,000

(if + savings of new system) or
(if – additional costs of the new system)

Figure 9.3.

designed so that the computer is able to accept all inputs whenever they occur, analysis is predicated on an assumption that all units, terminals, lines, disks, central processor(s), etc. are fully operational and performing as specified by the computer manufacturer. Unfortunately, machines never function properly all of the time. The period of time during which a system (computer, auxiliary storage units, terminals, lines, etc.) is working satisfactorily and is available to the customer for processing of information is called "system availability." System availability is equal to the total required available time minus the total of all the time needed for

    (a) scheduled (preventative) maintenance,

    (b) unscheduled system unavailability (down time), and

    (c) engineering changes.

Malfunctions occurring during the operation of a real-time system can have a direct and abrupt effect upon the daily operations of a business. In an instant, access to information stored within the computer can stop. The problem is compounded for the following reasons:

    (a) There is no written copy of the transaction, in machine intelligible form, and in the event of a computer malfunction, transactions can be lost. In fact, there is no record of a transaction, available to the computer, until it is stored on secondary storage.

    (b) Transactions enter the system in any sequence. Since programs can be executed at any moment, it can be difficult to determine the status of the system at the time of the malfunction.

    (c) The inputs are time dependent—that is, the information is needed immediately. Excessive delays reduce the value of the information because people are waiting for the output processed transactions at their terminals.

There are two types of equipment malfunctions: abrupt (immediately stopping all processing) or partial (intermittent signals of a condition which can be corrected only with human intervention). The latter results in a degraded level of service as it is the type of malfunction affecting a single component thus only reducing the thruput of the system.

Two examples of abrupt failures are:

    (a) a surge of electrical current sufficient to automatically cut off power to the computer system, and

    (b) a processor detection of incorrect parity.

Intermittent failures are:
- (a) reading of invalid data, which can be corrected without human intervention, and
- (b) loss and/or distortion of data caused by faulty communication lines.

Equipment malfunctions affect the flow of information to the operating departments. There must, therefore, be included in the design of a real-time system procedures to provide continuous data processing services. The analysis required is divided into:

1. Fallback—the specification of procedures necessary to permit continuous processing during periods of either abrupt or gradual equipment failure.
2. Recovery—once the equipment is capable of processing, procedures for again bringing information into the system so that the data are as current as if there had been no equipment failure.

FALLBACK PROCEDURES

In order to specify fallback procedures the systems analyst must first classify all possible combinations of failures. Since the procedures for supplying data processing services vary depending on whether a failure is abrupt or intermittent, there must first be an understanding of the effect of a malfunction. Again, when an abrupt failure takes place, everything stops. An intermittent malfunction involves a decision— that is, at what point are the number of errors greater than what can be considered tolerable for correct processing thus requiring the unit to be taken off-line for repairs. A single input message that is garbled because of a burst of noise on the line is not an intermittent malfunction. If, however, every other message cannot be "understood" by the computer, the frequency of the failure is such that corrective action is required.

The analyst must next determine the effect of each possible failure upon the functioning of the company. He must determine what the consequences (costs) are to the business if some, or all, of the information that is stored within the computer system is no longer available to operating personnel. Will the company lose a customer if an inquiry cannot be answered? What is the cost to the company if no orders can be filled and shipped for 24 hours because of unavailability of the Central Processing Unit? It is from management that the analyst can determine which situations cannot be tolerated. Each type of malfunction is reviewed to determine the estimated frequency of occurrence. The analyst must also ascertain the probability of each malfunction (the mean time to failure). Mean time to failure is an estimate of the number of hours that a given unit will perform in accordance with the manufacturer's specifications before a malfunction (performance below standards) will occur. These statistics are developed, by the equipment manufacturer from information obtained from internal tests as well as data obtained from users. As an example, it is possible that one of the components of a real-time system has a mean time to failure of 300 hours. If the estimated time for repair and bringing the unit back on-line is 4 hours (these 4 hours are also an average and include customer engineer traveling time), the analyst must determine the following:

1. Do the 4 hours that the unit is not available to the system represent a full or partial system failure? He must take into consideration that there will be times when (a) several units, all at the same time, are not functioning properly, and (b) as soon as one unit is repaired another unit may need to be taken off-line. There are probabilities of occurrence of each of these situations.

2. How does the loss of a unit for this period of time affect the user? Will there only be a delay or will sales be lost, expensive mistakes made, thus representing an additional cost of doing business?

3. Are there alternate procedures which can be instituted in order to minimize the effect of each possible malfunction. There are several methods of substituting an unavailable unit(s). The utilization of additional equipment, supplemental programs, and/or manual procedures are techniques that can be used individually or in combination.

Utilization of Additional Equipment. This consists of specifying additional information and/or be capable of performing the same functions (duplexing). In the event of a malfunction of one unit, requests would be rerouted manually or automatically to the other. The probability of both units malfunctioning simultaneously are substantially less than the probability of the malfunction of a single unit.[4] When simultaneous malfunctions do occur, the effect upon the system will, of course, be the same as the malfunction of a single unit in a nonduplexed environment.

Supplemental Programs. This involves the specification of special

---

[4] Probability of simultaneous malfunctions can be determined from any text on Probability Theory, *An Introduction to Probability Theory and its Application,* William Feller, Vol 1, J. Wiley & Sons, New York, 1957.

routines which, once a partial malfunction takes place, will perform one or more of the following:

(a) process only the more important transactions;
(b) send to various terminal locations messages to initiate prespecified fallback procedures; and/or
(c) modify existing routines, bypassing requests from/to unavailable units.

Introduction of Manual Procedures. These are specifications of techniques to record and/or manually process transactions which can no longer be accepted by the computer system. These consist of

(a) the manual recording of transactions,
(b) the rerouting of transactions, and
(c) the utilization of reports produced specially for the manual processing of transactions.

Representative fallback procedures are described in Table 9.4 for a simplex system. Table 9.5 reviews fallback procedures for a duplexed configuration.

TABLE 9.4 Simplex System Malfunctioning

Unit	Fallback Procedure
a. The central processing unit	All messages are saved for future entry into the system. Operating personnel will use and update previously produced reports/forms.
b. The line control unit	Same as for a.
c. The line control channel	Same as for a.
d. One or more disk drives	Transactions requiring information from that disk(s) are queued on another unit. Processing waits until the malfunctioning disk drive(s) is working properly. During the time that the disk(s) is not operational, messages are sent to all terminals to notify them of the malfunction.
e. Disk channel	Transactions requiring information from disk drives attached to the channel are handled in the same manner as d above.
f. One or more tape drives	If the drive is used for the logging of all real-time activity, input transactions are either: 1. logged on an alternative tape or disk unit, or 2. punched on cards. Drives used for intermediate stages of sorting are not a problem except that an alternate working storage area is required.

TABLE 9.4 (Continued)

Unit	Fallback Procedure
g. Tape channel	Same as for tape drive malfunction except transfers are made to a unit on another channel.
h. The printer, the punch card reader	Data to be printed or punched is transferred to an auxiliary storage unit. Control information required for calling in batch or special routines is entered via the console typewriter or a real-time terminal.
i. One or more terminals	Messages from malfunctioning terminal(s) will be transferred to another terminal for entry into the system. Output messages are returned to the station from which the messages were entered into the system. One of the functioning terminals can notify the system as to which terminals are not on-line or the computer can keep track of those stations to which the computer cannot send messages. A special routine is used to reroute broadcast messages (output messages going to several locations) to one of the on-line stations.
j. One or more communication lines	If all communication lines are not operating properly the procedures are the same as for a malfunctioning line control unit. If there is at least one line functioning, messages will be transferred (by telephone or messenger) to the operative terminals. The operator will enter all messages; *not* in the order received but in accordance with preassigned priorities (most important messages first).
k. The console typewriter	Control information will be sent, and received by one of the terminals attached to the system.

Duplex System Malfunctioning

In a duplexed system when one unit malfunctions the procedure to be followed is to reroute the flow of information by either automatic or manual switching.

In the duplexed system shown in Figure 9.4 there are two units available to perform each function. If one malfunctions, the other is used. Many duplexed systems use one of the computers for non-real-time processing. Such a duplexed system works as follows. The examples show Line Control Unit 1 and CPU 1 are on-line available for real-time processing. All four disk drives are on-line as each of the two sets of

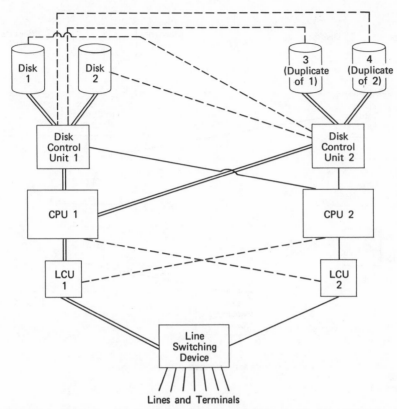

Figure 9.4. A representative fully duplexed system. The double line indicates data path (flow) for on-line system; solid line, data path (flow) for off-line system; dashed line, alternate path.

master records must be updated, so that each duplexed unit is an exact duplicate of the other. The internal data flow is via the double line path shown in Figure 9.4. In the event of a malfunction of Computer 1 the flow is rerouted as shown in Figure 9.5. The flow through the line control unit could be via LCU 1 or 2. Depending upon the procedure decided, in the event of a CPU malfunction, *both* the LCU and CPU can be switched. The same flexibility exists with the disk control units. All four drives could be accessed via only one of the control units. Better thruput can be obtained, however, by using, whenever possible, both disk control units.

A subsequent failure of the on-line LCU would cause a change to the flow in Figure 9.5 to that shown in Figure 9.6.

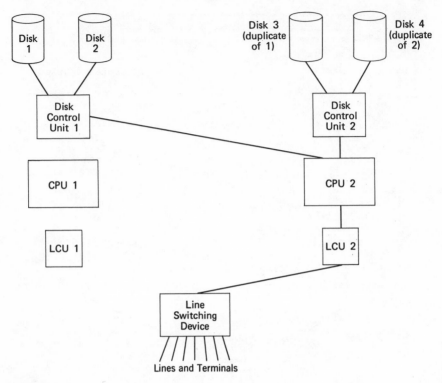

Figure 9.5

A subsequent malfunction of Disk Control Unit 1 would cause a modification in the flow to that shown in Figure 9.7. The flow can be re-routed to a "standard" route once the malfunctioning unit(s) is once again operational.

A malfunction of Disk 2 requires that all requests to Disk Unit 2 will have to be serviced solely by Disk Unit 4. The data that are stored on Units 2 and 4 can only be retrieved from Unit 4. As shown in Figure 9.8, the flow of data to (and from) Disk Drive 2 must be modified so that requests for records stored on Unit 2, which when updating records means a request for Unit 4 as well, are not allowed and are channeled as a single request to Unit 4. As long as one unit is available there is no loss of processing capability.

Once the analyst has specified fallback procedures, he must next determine how previously malfunctioning units are to be brought "on-line."

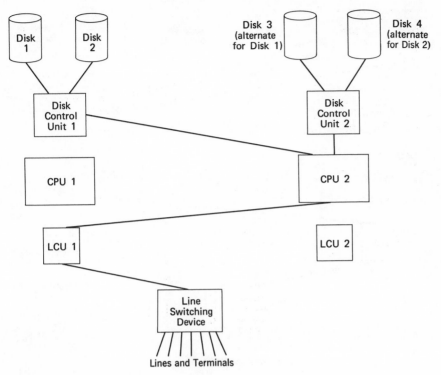

Figure 9.6

RECOVERY PROCEDURES

The specification of recovery procedures—that is, techniques for bringing the system to the condition it was prior to failure, must ensure that

(a) no master record(s) are updated twice by the same input transaction;

(b) messages originating during a system malfunction can be processed, preferably at the same time as the regular transactions are entering the system;

(c) no messages have been lost;[5] and

(d) any batch type programs that were interrupted because of the failure, are able to complete their run.

[5] An operator can determine which transactions have to be reentered if a sequential numbering system is a part of all input and output messages, thus permitting rapid detection of lost or not processed messages.

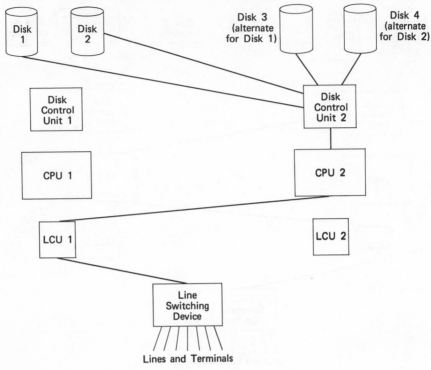

Figure 9.7

Representative recovery procedures for a simplex and a duplex system are shown in Table 9.5.

TABLE 9.5 Simplex System

Unit Being Brought On-Line	Recovery Procedure
a. The central processor	Since this is a total system failure the recovery procedures are:
	a. Initialize the system (since all information in core storage has been destroyed)
	b. Send a broadcast message to begin entering messages from the first unacknowledged transaction. A transaction is acknowledged only after it has been checked for correctness *and* logged.
	c. Backspace the tape message log and call in a special routine to determine if any disk records were destroyed or not updated.

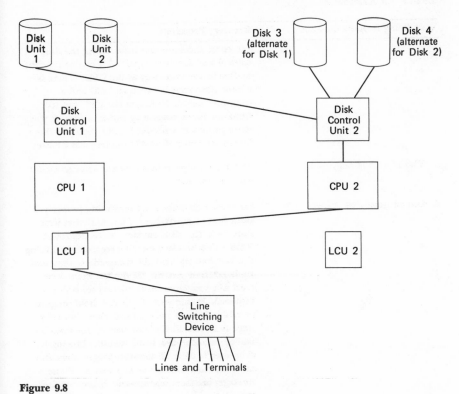

Figure 9.8

TABLE 9.5 (Continued)

Unit Being Brought On-Line	Recovery Procedure
	Records can be destroyed if the malfunction was abrupt and the failure occurred during the middle of writing a record onto disk storage.
	d. If the system permits concurrent batch processing, backspace the tape log to the last checkpoint read in the checkpoint with the operational program and continue processing. If there is no checkpoint the program will have to be rerun from the beginning. If a batch program had just completed all processing this will have been noted on the log. The next batch job can be read into the computer for processing.
b. The line control unit	A line control unit malfunction has the same effect upon real-time message processing as the failure of the main computer—no transactions

TABLE 9.5 (Continued)

Unit Being Brought On-Line	Recovery Procedure
	can enter and none can leave. Once the line control unit has been repaired it can be brought on-line in the same way as the CPU. There is a basic difference between an LCU and a computer failure is that, as the CPU can still function, batch processing can continue. If the main processor is needed for the repair of the line control unit the CPU can be taken off-line.
c. The LCU channel	The recovery procedures are the same as for the line control unit.
d. One or more disk drives	Once the disk units are functioning properly it must first be ascertained if any data that were stored on the disk surfaces were destroyed. That which was lost must be reconstructed using the last backup and all transactions that had updated those records. (If the lost areas were used as a scratch or work area no reloading is required. If that part of the disk held programs or tables that are not updated, then they only have to be reloaded.) The backup file must be loaded onto the disk to be rebuilt. The log is then searched for all messages logged since the last time the disk file was duplicated. These messages are then reprocessed. If none of the records that were stored on the disk were destroyed, then unprocessed transactions that were queued for processing can be read into core storage, processed, and sent to their destination. After this is completed normal processing can continue—the system has "caught up." If this processing of queued transactions is taking place during a peak period it will take a while to "catch up" because of the total load. It may be advisable during such a peak period to process only high priority transactions and delay lower priority messages, such as inquiries.
e. Disk channel	The same recovery procedures as are applicable for disk drives can be used in the event of a disk channel malfunction. It is not necessary, however, to check for damaged disk surfaces/lost records.
f. Tape drive	If an alternate drive was used for tape logging, recovery consists of: 1. Continue using the alternate drive.

200

TABLE 9.5 (Continued)

Unit Being Brought On-Line	Recovery Procedure
	2. Mount the tape log onto another drive, unrewound, and write a tape mark on the reel.
	3. At the end of the real-time day, when the log is considered complete for that time period, there will be two reels of logged information. Merge the "old" and new tape reels to the last transferring all data from them on a new reel of tape. The "new" reel will now contain transactions for the same time interval as all other logs.
	If the alternate medium was punched cards [6] then these must be read into the system, via the card reader, in order to update the tape log. If the unit being brought on-line was used for sorting or as a work area the only action required is that the system be notified, via the console typewriter, that the unit is now available.
g. Tape channel	The same procedures apply as for recovery from a malfunctioned tape unit. The transfer of logging information is from disk, or cards, rather than from an alternate tape unit.
h. The printer, the punch or the card reader	The data that were temporarily stored on an auxiliary storage unit can be transferred for printing and/or punching. The system can be informed via the console typewriter that control information and data can now enter the system via the card reader.
i. One or more terminals	A message can be entered, via either the console typewriter or one of the terminal stations, that had not malfunctioned, that the stations which were inoperative are now ready to send and receive messages. A special routine can be used to adjust the polling list, reflecting the latest status of the terminal attached to the system.
j. One or more communication lines	The same action can be followed as is used for the terminals.
k. The console typewriter	One of the terminal units can enter a message notifying the system and the control program, that the console typewriter is now in working order.

[6] Punching information into punch cards is the least preferable method of recording transactions during a malfunction of the logging unit. Besides the fact that cards can get lost it takes less time to update the log from a secondary storage, tape or disk unit.

Duplex System

The recovery procedures in a duplex system are less complicated than those needed for a simplex configuration. This is because processing either continues or completely halts. If switchover is automatic there is only a momentary stopping of processing during fallback—none during recovery. Recovery procedures in a duplexed system are required for updating a disk that was off-line. Depending upon the malfunction, recovery consists of

(a) copying all lost records which can be accomplished by entering the track numbers to be copied, (the drive from which the data is to come and the unit to which it is to be transferred), into the system via the console typewriter; and

(b) then using all records that would have been updated on both units but were written only on one of the disk units to update the file.

On completion of this operation both files are up-to-date. Processing can continue on a normal basis. Depending on the cost of the equipment needed to duplex the system, it could be cheaper, when considering total implementation and maintenance costs, to have a duplexed system. Fallback and recovery procedures are simpler, system unavailability is reduced, and less special routines than are needed to support a simplex system are required. This in turn reduces implementation time.

DEVELOPING THE IMPLEMENTATION SCHEDULE

Just as a schedule was developed for the design of the real-time system so must one be made for its installation. The work necessary for the implementation of a real-time system cannot be organized efficiently nor adequately monitored unless a detailed plan is prepared. The same reiterations as occurred for the development of the Pert Network for the design of the system will also take place. Balancing the manpower required, the time available to complete all work and the money budgeted will require several revisions of the preliminary schedule. The implementation schedule can be used to modify original estimates of staffing, budget, and programming requirements. The new schedule in turn will specify the delivery dates for the various components of the system.

The major items to be included in a real-time system implementation schedule are

(a) programmer education and training,
(b) development of programming documentation standards,
(c) writing of detailed operational program specifications, flow charting, decision table logic checkouts, coding, and testing of all operational routines,
(d) development of programming conventions,
(e) development of test data,
(f) specification of special system macros, support, and utility routines,
(g) analysis of computer-manufacturer supplied programs, such as operating systems and utility programs,
(h) if applicable, the conversion of presently running "batch" programs,
(i) site planning and preparation,
(j) development of terminal operator manuals and procedures; and
(k) training of terminal operators.

These eleven items represent *major* areas of work. Each summarizes many detailed items. Specification of special system macros, support, and utility routines, for example, can be further broken down as follows:

1. Specification of Special System Macros (It may be that after investigation of the macros supplied by the computer manufacturer that some of them can be used; thus reducing the macros to be written by the implementation group. Specification of the macros that are needed is the first step.)

   (a) Set switches macro.
   (b) Set timer to macro.
   (c) Wait macro.
   (d) Exit macro.
   (e) Link macro.

2. Support and Utility Routines
   (a) Data generator.
   (b) Environmental simulator; used to simulate data being received from the lines—required during the first stages of application program testing.
   (c) Clear disk routine.
   (d) Load disk program.
   (e) Copy data routine (from one unit to another).

It is important that the implementation schedule contain *all* the items necessary for the installation of the system. A complete list of all areas permits a more accurate measurement of progress once implementation has begun. A Pert Network developed prior to the beginning of implementation becomes a *working document*. It is updated as time passes to reflect the status of the study and is modified whenever there is additional information concerning new requirements or changes.

The completion of the implementation schedule is the last phase of the system design effort. Documentation of the information developed and *conclusions* made should now be completed. If, however, the study team was large enough, most of this documentation may have already be finished. This "final" system documentation is used to

(a) prepare, in one volume, all the information that will be the basis for implementing the system,

(b) ensure that all phases of the design effort have been documented,

(c) permit a complete review by management,

(d) supply a detailed background of the system to any new people hired for implementing the system.

The most immediate use of this documentation is for presentation to management and the steering committee. Final study can be prepared in two volumes. One, consisting of basically a summary of the new system, its costs, thruput, savings, and advantages, is for management. The other is for those who are interested in a greater level of detail and contains the information collected and developed by the real-time systems design group.

The first page of the documentation is a letter of transmittal. It is addressed to management and the steering committee and presents in a few paragraphs the material to follow. It is signed by the project manager and includes a distribution list. Next is the title page followed by a table of contents. The rest of documentation is usually divided into four sections.

Section 1 contains:

1. A general introduction of the new system and includes

(a) a generalized schematic of the configuration and

(b) the advantages of the new system, including displaceable costs.

2. The configuration of new system with a detailed list of equipment including the capabilities of each unit. Alongside each is the monthly rental (or cost if it is purchased) of each.

3. The processing capabilities of the system (thruput). Included should be

(a) the present transaction volumes,

(b) a list of new types of transactions,

(c) the projections of all transaction volumes to the year previously specified by the steering committee, and

(d) the time(s) of occurrence and composition of all peak periods.

Section 2 consists of:

1. A list of all assumptions, including their source, upon which the design of the real-time was based.

2. How each transaction will be processed by the system.

3. Real-time operational program specifications.

4. A list of all terminal locations and the messages entering and leaving each station.

5. Description of the characteristics and capabilities of the programs provided by the computer manufacturer.

6. A list of all transaction types and the formats of each.

7. Auxiliary storage requirements. Listed are all records to be stored as well as

(a) the information (fields) contained in each record,

(b) the rate growth of each file (of records),

(c) the total amount of auxiliary storage required, the types of units required, and what will be contained in each unit, as well as the amount of storage needed for data records, programs, tables, indexes, or reserved for future use.

8. Fallback and recovery procedures.

9. The implementation schedule, including staffing requirements, and estimated implementation costs.

Section 3 consists of results of all simulations (or analysis accomplished by analytic techniques) as well as:

1. Details of the models with the blocks used, and the time or volumes assigned to each.

2. Various input rates tested.

3. Thruput of the system.

4. Utilization of each of the components of the system and the queues developed at each of the units.

5. Response times.

6. Assumptions used in the simulation/analysis of the system.

Section 4 contains:

1. The functional specifications specifying the scope of the system study.

2. Reports of all interviews and meetings.
3. Reports of all existing problems.
4. The documentation of existing procedures.

PRESENTING THE SYSTEM TO MANAGEMENT

The above documentation should be used to support the formal presentation of the new system to management. Although the verbal presentation may take only a day, several weeks can pass before management's final approval of the new system. There will be questions to be answered. There may be requests for changes to the design. Major changes require a substantial redesign of the system. Any redesign delays the start of the implementation of the system. It may be that only some of the applications are approved, and the others deferred. This also could require a redesign of the system. If the real-time system truly fulfills the needs of the company in a more efficient manner and/or at a lower cost, management will authorize implementation of the new system.

CONCLUSION

The first job after the specification of the system components is to determine if the system can maintain the level of processing required. If improvement is required then one or more components of the system will have to be redesigned. Once the system meets performance requirements the following must be completed:

1. Estimate the savings as well as the costs of the new system, developing the projected total savings (or additional expenses).
2. Develop and document alternate procedures for processing during periods of system unavailability.
3. Develop an implementation schedule.
4. Using as a basis the documentation developed to date, prepare a final study report.
5. Present the new system to management.

The rewards of a thorough, well-planned real-time system design effort will be found in the implementation of the system. Problems will occur and changes will need to be made, but they will be minimal compared to the problems that can arise when implementing an improperly designed system.

CHAPTER 10

Installing a Real-Time System

REAL-TIME SYSTEMS ARE COMPLICATED AND DIFFICULT TO INSTALL. ALTHOUGH THERE ARE REAL-TIME SYSTEMS WHICH ARE DESIGNED FOR SEQUENTIAL HANDLING AND PROCESSING—THAT IS, ONE TRANSACTION RECEIVED, PROCESSED AND OUTPUTTED, WITH MINIMAL OVERLAP CAPABILITY, THIS CHAPTER REVIEWS THE ACTIVITIES INVOLVED IN THE SUCCESSFUL INSTALLATION OF THE MORE COMPLICATED REAL-TIME SYSTEMS; THOSE DESIGNED TO ACCEPT AND PROCESS A MULTITUDE OF SIMULTANEOUSLY INPUTTED TRANSACTIONS.

When planning the implementation of a real-time system, there are several factors which are of major importance in such an undertaking. They include the following:

1. The need for sophisticated special system support programs, testing routines, fallback, and recovery routines as well as terminal operator training programs (routines for training operating personnel in the usage of the new real-time terminals).
2. Servicing, in addition to the "standard" card reader, punch, printer tapes, and disk drives, many types of remote units, such as graphic units, typewriters, voice answer back, and line control unit(s). Intricate and involved programming is needed to support these devices. In addition, in a real-time system there will be many routines which must interact with each other and with many pieces of hardware as well as with a sophisticated supervisory control system.
3. Because of the complexity of multiprogramming, many more possibilities for program errors exist.
4. In most instances a real-time system is a new approach to data processing, for both operating personnel and programmers, many of whom have little prior experience in this field. A new approach is required. Such adjustment requires extensive training over a prolonged period.
5. More personnel are needed to install a real-time system than a batch type system using the same size computer configuration. This requires tight control and effective coordination. The project man-

ager must be alert to critical situations so that he can take prompt corrective action. This in turn requires good communications between the members of the implementation group as well as the group and the project manager.

Because of these factors as well as the scope and complexity of such an undertaking, the installation of a real-time system is somewhat formalized in nature. The efforts involved in the installation of a real-time system have therefore been subdivided into eight major phases.[1]

1. Forming the organization.
2. Training the implementation team.
3. Freezing the specifications.
4. Checking program logic.
5. Programming.
6. Testing.
7. Program documentation.
8. Cutting over the system.

It should be noted that although items 4, 5, 6, and 7 will take place sequentially for each program, not all programs will be in the same phase of development at the same time. This is because the time scheduled for each of these four steps can vary. Some of the factors affecting the time required for checking the program logic, programming, testing, and documentation are

(a) the complexity of the logic,
(b) the number and previous experience of the people assigned,
(c) the availability of test time,
(d) the extent that the programmers are involved in the conversion of presently running "batch type" systems,
(e) the completeness and accuracy of the program specifications, and
(f) the scheduled start date of the first step (checking the logic) of each application may not be the same.

FORMING THE ORGANIZATION

The study team designing a real-time system is organized functionally. The analysts represent the lowest level in the chain of command, and

---

[1] Two excellent books covering, in detail, real-time system implementation are:
Martin, J., *Programming Real-Time Computer Systems*, Prentice Hall, Englewood, N.J., 1965.
Head, R., *Real-Time Business Systems*, Holt, Rinehart, and Winston, N.Y., 1964.

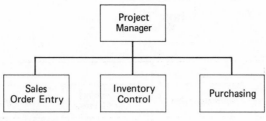

Figure 10.1

report directly to the project manager. The analysts are initially divided into groups, each of which is assigned to one application. See Figure 10.1.

As the analysis and documentation of the existing procedures for each of the applications are completed, the analysts are given other assignments, such as organization of the files, specifications of terminals, analysis of the control program requirements, and the like. Management approval of the new system generates an increase in the number of people assigned and the beginning of a period of many diverse operations which require close coordination. The requirements of a real-time system installation call for a change in organizational structure. Figure 10.2 is a representative chart of a real-time system implementation effort. The tasks to be accomplished are divided among the members of the implementation team, each having, in addition to completing his assignment on schedule, the following responsibilities:

1. Project Manager—his duties remain basically the same as those required for the design effort, namely
   (a) responsibility for the implementation of the system in accordance with the requirements specified by the steering committee,
   (b) review and approval of all major decisions and changes made/requested by the implementation group and the steering committee, and
   (c) responsibility for the progress of the implementation.

2. Standards Group—
   (a) develop programming conventions,
   (b) specify documentation standards,
   (c) ensure that all standards and conventions are conformed to,
   (d) develop system test data,[2] and

---

[2] System test data are transactions specially prepared by the standards group as a part of their responsibility to ensure that all programs will be fully tested.

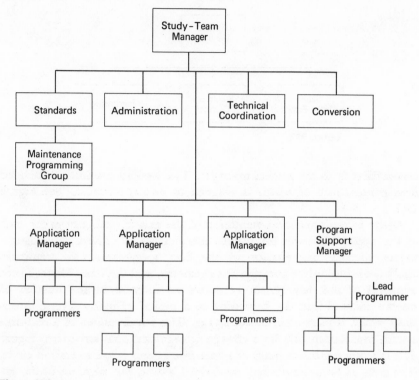

Figure 10.2

(e) maintain the integrity of the system.[3]

3. Administration—

   (a) ensure that all information submitted is typed according to prescribed formats,

   (b) order all approved materials requested by the implementation group,

   (c) responsible for the distribution of all materials received,

   (d) is aware of the present location and status of important items,

   (e) schedules test time on the basis of predetermined priorities.

---

[3] System integrity is ensured, if the programs that are being added to the library of fully tested routines do not interfere with or cause problems to these already debugged programs. Although a program may have successfully been tested on its own (on a stand-alone basis), it may still create problems (bugs) when coupled with other routines. This can happen for example when a programmer utilizes registers or macros which are not supposed to be used.

4. Technical Coordination—coordinates the work of the implementation group with
   (a) engineering staff responsible for computer and terminal site preparation,
   (b) representatives of the common carrier,
   (c) representatives of the equipment manufacturer(s) as related to delivery dates, on-site testing, etc.,
   (d) training of the implementation staff as well as the operating personnel.
5. Application Manager—responsible for the development of program logic, coding, testing, and documentation of all routines required for the running of the assigned applications.
6. Program Support Manager—Responsible for the specification, coding, documentation, etc. of all special support routines required by the implementation of the system.
7. Conversion Manager—responsible for the conversion of all files as well as the coordination of all areas necessary for the parallel operation of both systems, manual and real-time, and the eventual phasing out of the manual system.

Once the organization has been defined and the schedule for when these positions will be filled has been determined, the implementation can begin the second phase—training the implementation team.

TRAINING THE IMPLEMENTATION TEAM

Those not fully familiar with the new system will have to be instructed in the details of how the system is to function. The training should consist of three sections: (1) a general review of the system, its operation and personnel assignments; (2) a detailed examination of all documentation (the final study report) related to the new system; and (3) a study (for *all* team members) covering the implementation schedule, the organization (chain of command), and work assignments as well as areas of specification. If required, the final part of the training consists of sending team members to school. If the team is large enough a special class, at the customer's site, can be arranged. School encompasses formal training in the following areas:

1. Program language; which includes instruction set, macro writing, coding and debugging techniques and sample problems which are run on a computer.
2. Operating system; features, options.

3. Line control programming.

4. Utility program specifications.

5. Disk and tape concepts.

Once school is completed, actual work can begin. The first step is the expansion of the operational program logic—initially into detail program specifications, and then into flow charts. The difference between operational program logic, detail program specifications, and flow charting is the amount of detail contained in each. Operational program logic specifies the functions to be performed. Detail program specifications describe how and enumerates the sequence in which these functions are to be performed. Flow charts which expand each function in greater detail are drawn just prior to the initiation of coding. The amount of detail in the flow charts should be such that the routine can be coded with no other knowledge of the application. Because of the complexity of the logic of many real-time routines, prior to flow charting, the logic of the routine should be checked by means of decision tables.

FREEZING THE SPECIFICATIONS

No matter how good, or complete, the system design, the project manager will constantly be requested to make changes to system functions. He must carefully evaluate these requests. Those which cause a major change to the system; for instance, a new application which increases the number of on-line files must be refused if they consequently necessitate a redesign of the system. Minor changes, on the other hand, can be permitted.

A point is reached during the implementation when all specifications must be considered unchangeable. The project manager must inform all concerned at what point no more changes can be made *and he must insist that that date be adhered to.* Beyond this point, even a minor change can cause a major delay to the installation. For example, a request is made for the addition of one field, customer's sales, for the last year to be added to one of the output messages. This field must be added to the customer's record. The addition of one field before programming began would be only a minor modification, but the same request occurring in the middle of programming could cause the following:

1. Modification to the punching document—the addition taking place after some of the documents have been filled out. Assuming that

there is space on the punching document, the new field must be added to all those documents that have already been filled out.

2. Changes to specifications and additional coding added to the "edit checking" routines. The routines must match the new field in correctness and must be changed so that the field can be inserted in the customer's record. All routines that have been coded must be modified. Imagine how much greater the impact on the work done to date would be if the change is made once the real-time system is in final testing. Again, it is the duty of the project manager to inform all concerned at what point in time no more changes can be made.

CHECKING PROGRAM LOGIC

A program is a list of instructions to be executed in a computer to achieve previously specified results. The directions to a program of what to do when confronted with certain situations is the logic of the program. Before beginning the coding, the logic should be checked to see if it is accurate as well as complete. It should include directions for program performance in every possible situation. It is much more difficult and time consuming to identify and correct omissions in logic once the program is being tested. It becomes difficult to check the logic of a complex routine when reviewing flow charts because

(a) many pages are needed, thus requiring the reader to jump from one page to another, and

(b) flow charts combine and interleave techniques used when coding (load registers, format fields, arithmetic operations, etc.) with the logic of the routine.

Decision tables are a tabular technique recommended for documenting logic.[4] They have been designed in a manner that, when correctly used, even the most complex logic can be shown clearly and followed with ease. Omissions and inconsistencies can be quickly noted. Decision tables permit a check on the logic of the routine even by a person unfamiliar with the purpose of the program.

As the logic becomes more complicated, the value of checking and planning the logic by means of decision tables increases.

PROGRAMMING

Because of the complexity of real-time programming, this section should only be considered a general review of the subject. The pro-

[4] For a detailed review of decision tables, see Appendix B.

gramming of routines for a real-time system is more time consuming than the programming of similar routines for a batch type system, because there are many more restrictions placed upon the real-time programmer when coding his program. These restrictions consist of the following:

1. The requirements that any code that is produced be "reentrant." [5]
2. The techniques that permit a linking of application routines with
   (a) each other,
   (b) the operating system,
   (c) line control routines, and
   (d) system macros.
3. Limitations on size, the type of coding permitted, the maximum number of positions of storage, and/or the processing (execution) time.

To introduce order to the implementation effort of many programmers whose programs must all interact, Interface Programming Conventions are documented and distributed to each programmer. The relationship of these documents to the others that the programmers will be using is shown schematically in Figure 10.3. The initial distribution is prepared by the administration group and distributed to each programmer before he begins his detail flow charting. As work continues, each programmer will receive additional internal programming requirement releases. The programmer, in turn, may be submitting to the standards group programming requirements that he wishes to be adopted by all the programmers so that his program can function. Once any of these conditions for coding are approved by the standards group they are released to all the programmers. The approval of new internal program requirements may require changes to existing routines. If the program has not been released to the maintenance programming group, the programmer, if necessary, has to change his coding. Released routines will have to be changed by the maintenance programmers and retested.

[5] Reentrant coding as mentioned previously is a technique which permits several transactions to be in varying stages of processing, in a multi-programmed environment, all of which are able to use the *same* copy of the routine. This is accomplished by conforming to the *additional* restraints of: (1) no switches set *within* the routine, and (2) no counters or accumulations permitted within the routine. This is achieved by means of setting aside a section of core storage for *each* transaction in which switches, counters, etc. are stored and set.

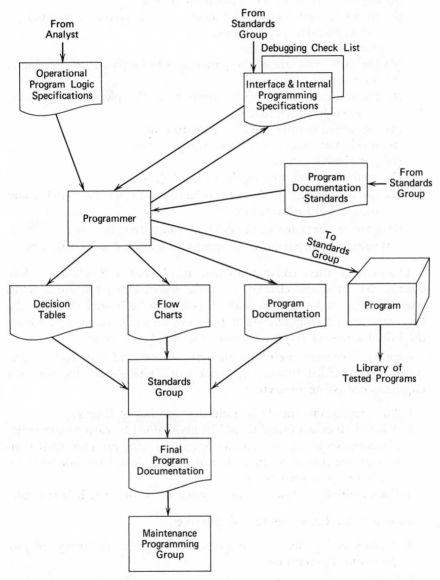

Figure 10.3

Programming conventions include such items as

(a) registers available for application coding,

(b) contents, and usage, of registers not available (reserved) to the application programmer,

(c) macros available for use,

(d) the order and size of the parameters to be passed to the macro,

(e) the purpose of the macro,

(f) the location (label-register address) of the parameters (results) received from the macro,

(g) maximum permissible size of the routine,

(h) maximum execution time of the program,

(i) permissible labels,

(j) methods for requesting data record(s),

(k) size and format of the area to be used to store the switches and counters of each routine,

(l) how to access any of the fields of a data record,

(m) names, and functions, performed by standard error routines.

The more of these conventions that are defined and released before coding, the fewer the changes (to these conventions) required. This, plus the other duties of the standards group, make it advisable that the most experienced programmers and analysts be a part of, at least during the initial stages of implementation, the standards group.

Another document useful for the preparation and approval of programs is a Standard Debugging Check List. This should include such requirements as the following:

1. All compilations should include the printing of listings.

2. A log of all errors found should be maintained by each programmer.

3. No out-of-sequence tags on any program listing are permitted (out-of-sequence should mean that cards in the deck have not been inserted in the correct place).

4. Document the purpose of each switch when the switch is created.

Such a check list serves several purposes.

1. It trains and guides new programmers in the correct usage of programming conventions.

2. It reduces the tendency to take "short-cuts." These apparent time-savers eventually create problems in that operating personnel are liable to lose track of nonapproved (unconventional) operating procedures.

The adoption of these guidelines will not only reduce time required to write programs but also minimize the initial interference of one routine with another. Routines which are coded separately by programmers, working more or less independently of one another, must work together as parts of a total system. It is to minimize the effects of changes on these programs that these internal requirements must be rigidly adhered to. Because of the dynamic nature of real-time applications, there *will be* changes to the system. With the passage of time the configuration will need to be changed because of the addition of new equipment. New restraints (changes) will be required to existing routines because of the planned addition of new applications. Modifications and improvements to "fully" tested routines are part of the responsibilities of the maintenance programming group.

TESTING

Programs that work in a complete time-dependent environment are difficult to debug. Some of the conditions that cause program malfunctions are the following:

1. Peak period conditions: During peak periods
   (a) if extended processing takes place it could result in the loss of part of an input message (the system did not give the line control program enough time to store incoming characters).
   (b) if more than one transaction requires the same data record it could cause a loss of information and/or incorrect results.

2. Different types of transactions when either entering, leaving, or in the midst of processing, in combination, may cause errors in results. Transactions in combination may result in errors because all, for example, may utilize the same index registers at the same time, one transaction thus destroying the information or addresses of the other.

3. Equipment malfunctions may, if they occur during certain parts of the processing, introduce errors. A disk drive malfunction occurring during a write operation could cause the loss of record, because the part of main computer memory containing the record may be released for other purposes despite the fact that the record has been destroyed on the disk.

Because of the many types of errors that can take place, a systematic formula has evolved for the testing of programs that must work in a real-time environment—the "building block" approach. This procedure attempts to ensure that programs are first fully "debugged" in a set of conditions of minimal complexity before introducing the conditions that will be testing for more difficult to detect errors. Testing takes place first in a artificial (simulated) environment, thus eliminating errors that could be caused, for example, by distortions on communication lines. Thus, when an error takes place the number of possible sources is reduced. Once all routines have been fully tested in these simulated conditions, the programs are again tested with the actual equipment. The units are attached to the system on a gradual basis. Thus if any errors take place, the possible causes have been pinpointed, theoretically at least, to conditions caused by either the newly introduced equipment or the routines using the equipment.

There are four parts to testing by this method:

1. Individual routine testing.
2. Testing in a simulated environment.
3. Testing with actual equipment—no lines or terminals.
4. Testing with all equipment.

INDIVIDUAL ROUTINE TESTING

The first tests, after a clean compilation has been obtained, are intended to get the loops out of the program and to make it run its full course—that is, until it completes its processing properly. These first tests involve test data loaded into the files, and the real-time transactions entering the system, not from the terminal and line control unit, but via a tape or disk drive.

There are several types of testing aids/programs which can be of use during this as well as during subsequent phases of testing. Some of these are as follows:

(a) Macro Trace—these traces print preselected data when encountering execution of prespecified macros. For example, every time an ADD instruction is encountered, the contents of the fields before and after the additions are either printed or written on auxiliary storage for subsequent printing. The specifications for these routines should include the ability to initiate their execution from either the card reader or the console typewriter.

(b) Branch Trace—this type of trace will print out the locations to which the program is routed whenever a branch instruction is encountered.

(c) Selective Core Dumps—on completion or at the selected point in the processing of each transaction, prespecified sections of core storage are printed.

(d) Message Logging Routine—all messages, input and output are logged. They are then printed together with all fields that have been changed by the routine being tested. Once volume testing begins, such techniques are helpful in reducing the large volume of results that must be checked.

TESTING IN A SIMULATED ENVIRONMENT

1. Single Thread Testing—This next step is to test several routines that have successfully completed individual debugging on the following basis:

(a) All segments of the routine to be core resident—that is, no sub-routine call in from secondary storage. If the final configuration is a duplexed system this stage uses only simplexed equipment.

(b) One transaction entering the system at a time. Once the routines have been fully tested—that is, tested under these conditions with the data developed by the standards group, they are tested again under conditions which permit program and sub-routines call-in from secondary storage—under control of the operating system. If a "debugged" operating system is available the programs can be tested working together with these control routines. If no operating system is available the control programs will also have to be simulated.

2. Multi-thread Testing—This step, introduces testing of several transactions simultaneously, entering, being processed, and leaving the system. At this stage, entering and leaving consists of transactions coming in from and being written on auxiliary storage. It should be noted that as the testing progresses from one stage to the next the *number* of errors should be decreasing. Each remaining error, being more complex, will be more difficult to find and correct.

TESTING WITH ACTUAL EQUIPMENT—NO LINES OR TERMINALS

The delivery of additional equipment, any duplexed units, and the line control unit(s) should have been scheduled to coincide with the beginning of this phase of program testing. As each additional unit is connected the programs should again be tested still using only test transactions and file data—first single thread, then on a multithread basis. The routines should also be checked under conditions of equipment failure and fallback, as well as recovery. The last unit to be attached should be the line control unit. The transactions now enter the system from an auxiliary storage unit or another computer. This is accomplished by connecting a second computer to the line control unit in a manner similar to the connection which is made by a communication line. With this special computer hookup, transactions are sent from one computer to the other via the LCU. This technique permits the inputting of many transactions in a manner closely paralleling the way in which messages would be received from remote terminal locations. When errors occur, they will have to be analyzed to determine if they were caused by the new unit added to the system, the LCU, the sending unit or the program being tested.

TESTING WITH ALL EQUIPMENT

Once this phase of debugging has been completed, single thread testing starts again. This time, however, transactions are entered via terminals. Errors that occur now can be caused either by the programs themselves, the communication lines, and/or the terminals. New programs which enter testing after the equipment has been attached to the system must go through the same phases of testing. They must first be tested as if the equipment is not attached to the system. In this situation, various routines in different stages of testing will continue until all programs have been tested, even though the system may be operational—running with previously "cut over" applications. In order to minimize operator errors, the first on-line usage of the terminals should take place in the training mode.

The training mode is a technique for training operators while the system is operational *without* modifying the files. The mode is entered via the console typewriter, if it is a new terminal location, in order to update the polling list. The message is entered from the terminal itself for a location that is already being polled. Receipt of this transaction calls in a routine which will analyze input transactions and send output back to the terminal, making it appear to the new operator that the input was fully processed. Any format errors, invalid transaction codes, etc. will be "caught" by the computer. The training mode thus permits terminal operator training in a real environment without adversely affecting the system.

Thought and preparation must be given as to how the terminal operators are introduced to the equipment. It is very important that the operators receive a favorable impression on their first contact with the new system. Operators are frequently apprehensive in regard to the system and are concerned perhaps that they might not be able to master the new techniques necessary for the performance of their job. It is, therefore, important to make the operators feel confident and let them know that they are an essential part of the system and vital to the ultimate success of the system. It is they who must learn to use the system productively. An extensive and thorough training period is therefore required.

Once the operators have been instructed in the way the terminals are to be used, transactions can be entered to process and update files that contain special test data records. After each test the updated files can be checked by means of a routine which will compare all changed fields of the updated records with the records as they were prior to the test. Before each test the unmodified records can be moved from their own specially protected area into the area that will be used during the tests, thus making "new" records available at the beginning of each set of tests. These training sessions should continue until the terminal operators feel comfortable with their "new" terminals.

PROGRAM DOCUMENTATION

The documentation of all programs coded by the implementation team is a time-consuming, but important task. In order to standardize all program documentation, a Program Documentation Standards Manual should be prepared. It should specify all that is necessary to be documented as well as how the information should be formatted. There are five major sections. Listed below is each section with its related sub-sections.

1.0 Program Documentation
    1.1 Decision Tables
    1.2 Core—Secondary Storage Used
    1.3 Estimation Running Time
    1.4 Identification of Parameters, Table, etc.
    1.5 Entry Conditions
    1.6 Exit Conditions
    1.7 Error and Exception Detection
    1.8 Restrictions and Special Requirements

1.9 Switches—Usage—On and Off Meaning
1.10 Logic Description (High-Level Flow Chart)
1.11 Detailed Block Diagram
1.12 Listing of Test Data Used
1.13 Final Compilation

2.0 Data Record Specifications
   2.1 Summary of Data Records used by the program
   2.2 Assumptions (if any)
   2.3. Function—Used for
   2.4 Record Location (Disk/Tape)
   2.5 Cycling (when changed or updated)
   2.6 Addressing
   2.7 Record Layout
   2.8 Record Size
   2.9 Record Restrictions
   2.10 Cross References (when referred to in program)

3.0 Input Record Documentation
   3.1 Summary of Purpose, and Contents of the Input Record
   3.2 Input Media
   3.3 Input Transaction Formats
   3.4 Results of Input Receipt
   3.5 Record Description
   3.6 Cross References
   3.7 If Punched Card Input (punching documents, form, name and number)

4.0 Output Record Documentation
   4.1 Summary of Purpose and Contents of the Output Record
   4.2 Assumptions
   4.3 Output Media
   4.4 Type of Output Record (if Report—its name, number and who approved it outside of this department)
   4.5 Cross Reference (where referred to in the program)

5.0 Macros
   5.1 Summary of Purpose
   5.2 Usage (when needed)
   5.3 Calling Sequence
   5.4 Possible Returns
   5.5 Listing of Coding
   5.6 Examples of Usage

CUTTING OVER THE SYSTEM

Concurrent with the coding and testing of programs, it is necessary to convert all required data files from their present form and store them on auxiliary storage units. The actual loading of these files should be preceded by two parallel efforts—the preparation of the data and the coding of special file building routines. Preparation of data includes

(a) specification of the formats of all punching documents,
(b) training of personnel as to how to fill out the documents, the present location of files, and the order in which they are to perform their work,
(c) entering data into the punching documents, and
(d) punching of the data from the documents into punched cards.

Special file building routines consist of programs which will

(a) check the input data for errors,
(b) sort all data into the required sequence, and
(c) build (format) the records.

All routines must be specified, checked by means of decision tables, flow charted, coded, and then tested.

The special file building routines are used to create and load the data files. The building of the files continues until all data are on the files after errors and inconsistencies, located by the file building routines, have been corrected. Programs can now be tested with "live data records." The purpose of this phase of testing is not only to find errors in the programs but, of equal importance, also to locate errors whose source is "bad file data." The final phase of testing ushers in the parallel running of the system. Parallel running is the concurrent running of the old system and the real-time system. This is the final phase of system checking prior to the abandonment of the presently existing system. It is of utmost importance to locate as many errors as possible, in this phase, since the real-time system is entering transactions and updating files.[6] The running of both systems in parallel will continue until the real-time system is working satisfactorily; namely, that all differences between the results obtained by real-time processing and the presently existing system have been accounted for. Once the real-time system is running satisfactorily for a period of time (previously agreed upon by the parties concerned) the "old" system can be discarded.

---

[6] If serious problems are encountered, it may be advisable that all transactions necessary for maintaining the "currentness" of the files, be punched on cards (rather than entered via terminals which is slower) thus updating the files on a batch basis.

THE POST IMPLEMENTATION REVIEW

During the implementation and initial running of the first real-time application(s) information should be assembled for the purpose of improving the efficiency of future applications.

The types of information that should be collected are as follows:

1. The time required by each programmer for
   (a) flow charting,
   (b) coding, and
   (c) testing.
2. The number of times and the amount of machine time required for
   (a) compilations and
   (b) tests.
3. The types of errors found during various stages of testing.
4. The number and type of transactions that are processed by the system, as well as their time of occurrence.

Thus the project manager will be able to learn not only from mistakes that were made but he, as well as the entire implementation team, will be able to benefit from techniques and skills acquired from experience. In addition, information concerning the time required to complete the many items necessary for the implementation of the application(s) can be used for more accurate estimates of the time needed to perform these functions for the applications that will next be transferred to the real-time system.

An Example of a Simulation Program

In the chapter on simulation, Chapter 8, there was a brief discussion of the GPSS language and its use in modeling a real-time system. That discussion avoided the details of the way the simulator program operates. This appendix will give a more thorough explanation of the major functions of any simulator program, regardless of the language used. To illustrate their use, a sample simulator program will be outlined.

The descriptions of the functions and the samples are not meant to be exhaustive, but they will sufficiently demonstrate the type of activity that takes place in such a program. The major functions and bookkeeping areas are

1. Transaction Generator,
2. Random Number Generator,
3. Action Chain,
4. System Clock, and
5. Facility Status List

TRANSACTION GENERATOR

The first ingredient for a simulation is the logical model itself, which consists of a routing description of each transaction type, variable descriptions, and definitions of the physical units and tables. These constitute the input to the program. The simulator runs a sample of transactions through these specified routings and records the times spent by each transaction at key points in the system. The first function of the simulator, therefore, is to create transactions, a function that is called "transaction generation."

A transaction generator reserves an area of computer storage for each transaction. These areas will be used for storing information about the transactions' behavior during the simulation run. The exact nature of this information will be discussed when the sample program is explained.

225

RANDOM NUMBER GENERATOR

The second function required in a simulation program is a "random number generator." This enables the program to handle random variables in a special way. A random number is the technique used to pick one time from a distribution. Whenever a time, which is a variable, is required for application to a transaction, this time must be represented not as a "distribution" but as a specific value. For example, suppose the "tape write" time for a transaction type is as shown in Figure A.1. The probabilities are "cumulative"—that is, each position on the vertical axis represents the probability of the tape write time being less than or equal to the corresponding value on the horizontal axis. (If the probabilities were noncumulative, they would be 30, 50, 10, and 10). In order to assign a value to this variable as needed, a number from 0 to 100 is "picked" at random. If it is less than or equal to 30, the value 5 is assigned, if less than or equal to 80, the simulator assigns 10, etc.

How can the simulator "pick" a number within a computer program? Specifically, how can a *series* of numbers be generated such that there is a guarantee that no relationships exist among them? (This requirement must be met if the simulation is to represent a truly "random" sample for each variable.) Several techniques have been developed for generating sequences of random numbers. One of the older techniques is known as the "mid-square" method. Usually, a given number is multiplied by itself, producing a number twice the size. For example, the square of a six-digit number would be a twelve-digit number. Then the middle digits of the product are used as the new number to be

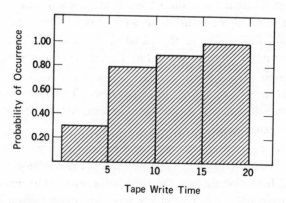

Figure A.1

multiplied. Each number in this sequence is unrelated [1] to its predecessor because of the sufficient randomness in the middle digits.

The prime consideration in designing a random number generator is the "period" of a given sequence. This refers to the number of items in the sequence that can be produced before the sequence repeats itself. For example, a sequence like 6, 17, 10, 65, 42, 6, 17, 10, 65, 42, . . . would have a period of 5. Once the first number of the sequence turns up again, it is obvious that the entire sequence must repeat itself, because the same computational technique is used in generating each number. The objective in designing any random number generator is to make the period as long as possible. The shorter the period, the less the randomness in the sequence. The period of 5 in the example above would be much too small because every number would be exactly equal to its fifth successor. In practice, by proper selection of starting numbers and of computational procedures for manipulating the sequence, experts have been able to generate sequences with periods over one million.

Another illustration might clear up any misunderstandings about the need for random number generation. Suppose we had a jar of 1000 marbles, 600 black and 400 red. If we wanted to take a random sample of marbles from this jar, we would certainly want to make sure that they were well mixed. If all the black marbles were on top, the sample would be all black and not representative of the whole "environment" of marbles in the jar. Similarly, in order to guarantee that we are drawing a truly representative sample from a given distribution for a variable, we need a random number generator to effectively "mix up the marbles."

ACTION CHAIN

The technique used by a simulator to maintain the status of transactions within the model is an "action chain," sometimes called an "event" or "move" chain. This chain is a set of entries maintained within computer storage which contains key information concerning each transaction. The following data are considered minimal for each transaction entry:

   (a) Transaction number,
   (b) Next move time,
   (c) Facility number, and
   (d) Transaction start time.

[1] A relationship between numbers can be illustrated by the sequence 3, 6, 12, 24, where each number is twice its predecessor.

The transaction number is internally generated for the purpose of keeping track of messages that have entered the model. The next move time of a transaction is the time at which the transaction is expected to attempt to proceed to the next point in its flow. Each time a transaction "moves" from one facility to another the entries are "rechained"—that is, a new position in the chain is determined for each entry.

The action chain is really two separate chains, one for those currently occupying facilities and the other for those currently waiting for facilities. These are called the Occupy Chain and the Wait Chain, respectively. Entries in the Occupy Chain are sorted by "next move time," whereas those in the Wait Chain are sorted by facility number. When rechaining takes place, therefore, entries may actually be moved from the Occupy to the Wait Chain or vice versa.

SYSTEM CLOCK

The system clock is the instrument in a simulation program which represents the passage of time in the real world. This is accomplished by reserving a small area which is initialized to zero to correspond to the "start" of the period to be simulated. Each time an "event" is to occur—that is, each time a transaction moves, this "clock field" is updated to correspond to the "next move time" of the transaction that is moving. The system clock is, therefore, a conceptual convenience—it always represents the time of the current event being processed in the simulator.

FACILITY STATUS LIST

The facility status list maintains continuous indication of the state of each facility defined in the input data. There is one entry for each facility, and the following information might be associated with each entry:

(a) Facility number
(b) Facility Status
    0 = free
    1 = busy
(c) Transaction number currently occupying
(d) Number of transactions waiting
(e) Total "busy time"

The amount of information provided in this list may vary, depending on the particular requirement and purpose of the simulation. (If the simulator has "storages" in addition to "facilities," as in GPSS, a slightly different bookkeeping procedure is needed).

Figure A.2 shows the basic structure of a flow chart for a "typical" simulation program. The chart does not include initialization and output but assumes that some transactions have already been generated (entered in the Action Chain) and assigned to facilities. At A, the Next Move Time for a transaction is to be determined, this transaction having just been assigned to a facility. Suppose the occupation time is a probability distribution which was presented to the program as one of the many "functions." In order to determine a particular time for this transaction, we generate a random number and "look up" its corresponding value as given in the table for this function. Then Next Move Time = CLOCK + Occupation Time, where CLOCK represents the time that this transaction is being assigned to the facility. The new Next Move Time replaces the old one for this transaction, which is then inserted in the appropriate position in the Occupy Chain.

The next step for the simulator is to update the CLOCK. There are three items which must be examined: (1) the minimum Next Move Time, which appears in the first entry in the Occupy Chain; (2) time when a new transaction is due to enter the system, which has been previously determined; and (3) the "end of run" time. The lowest of these three times becomes the new CLOCK time, and, depending on which one it is, the simulator takes one of three possible paths.

If the CLOCK was updated by an "end of run" condition, all processing of transactions is halted and a set of output procedures is begun. The exact nature of these procedures depends on the nature and purpose of the simulation run.

If the CLOCK was updated by facility release (Item 1) the simulator follows the path on the left side of the chart. First, the released facility is designated as "available" in the facility status list. Then, the Wait Chain is examined for transactions in queue behind this same facility, and an appropriate transaction is selected by means of any specified "priority rule." One rule might be "the transaction waiting the longest," another, "the transaction with the largest number of remaining operations." (If no transactions are currently waiting we skip immediately to C). The selected transaction is designated as occupying this facility; the Facility Status List is updated again, indicating the "busy" status for the facility, and a Next Move Time is determined for the transaction

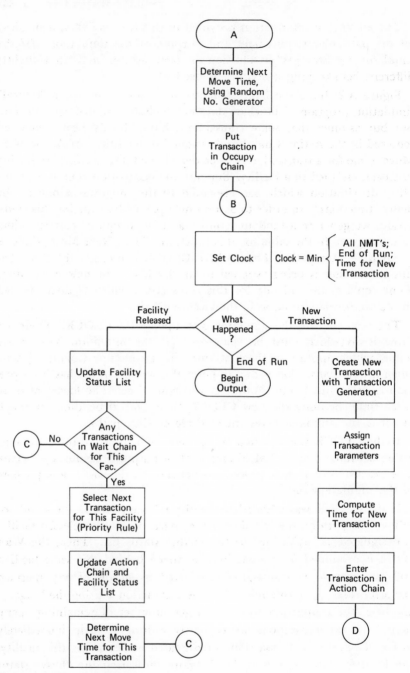

Figure A.2. Simulator flow chart.

230

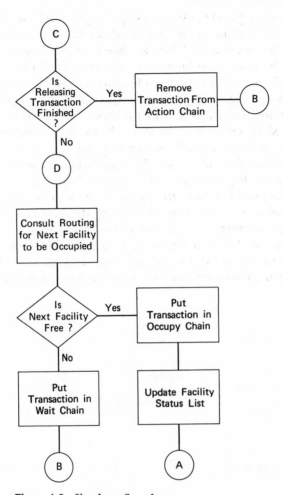

Figure A.2. Simulator flow chart.

being assigned to the facility. Finally, the transaction is placed in the Occupy Chain and the simulator moves to point C.

If the CLOCK was updated by a "new transaction" (Item 2), the simulator follows the path on the right side of the chart. The Transaction Generator allocates an area in storage for the new transaction with the appropriate fields and parameters. (In a real-time system simulation, one parameter would be "message type," which would be assigned to the transaction by consulting the "message type distribution" with the help of the Random Number Generator. Similarly, the input message, tape message, and output message lengths would be determined.) An entry in the Action Chain is created for this transaction, and the simulator moves to Point D. Then a "time for next transaction" is computed using the same techniques as in determining "next move times."

At Point C, we return to consideration of the transaction which originally released the facility when the CLOCK was last updated, if the update was indeed caused by a facility release. The releasing transaction is first checked to see if it is finished. If so, it is removed from the Action Chain and the program returns to point B. If not, the program moves to D, where the routing for this transaction is consulted to determine the next facility to be occupied. If this facility is free, the transaction entry is placed in the Occupy Chain (if it is not already there), the facility status list is updated to indicate the new facility is "busy," and the program returns to A. If the facility is not free, the transaction entry is placed in the Wait Chain, if it is not already there, and the program returns to B. If the original updating of the CLOCK was caused by a new transaction, this transaction is also processed at point D.

Decision Tables

A decision table is a technique for formalizing and documenting the logic of a program. Developing a decision table involves the division of a piece of paper into four sections, each section being separated by a double line. As shown in Figure B.1, the four sections are named; Condition Stub, Action Stub, Condition Entry, and Action Entry.

All possible situations liable to occur are entered in the Condition Stub. The Action Stub includes all the possible actions necessary to satisfy the conditions entered on the Condition Stub.[1] The Condition Entry lists the situations specifying the occurrence of the condition, in the form of Y (Yes), N (No) and Blank spaces (not applicable). The Action Entry specifies the action, or actions, to be taken for a given set of conditions. One or more indications, usually X's, entered in the Action Entry section, specifies the actions that are to be taken.

In order to show more clearly the manner in which a Decision Table is prepared, as an example the sequence of steps prior to coding the routine for processing "Receipt of a Customer's Order" will be reviewed.

---

[1] A decision table is generally not filled out in the sequence described herein. IBM General Information Manual, #F20-8102 entitled "Decision Tables—A Systems Analysis and Documentation Technique," contains techniques for filling out and reading decision tables as well as including modifications to tailor the table to specific usages.

CONDITION STUB	CONDITION ENTRY
ACTION STUB	ACTION ENTRY

Figure B.1. Schematic of a decision table.

The operational program logic specifications that were developed during the design of the system are:

OPERATIONAL PROGRAM LOGIC FOR RECEIPT OF
CUSTOMER'S ORDER

All transactions are to be checked for completeness. The items on the input transactions are to be matched with the inventory master record. If there is no master record, the input transaction is to be considered in error. For all transactions (where the master is found), the program is to update the inventory master record by:

1. Reducing the quantity on hand. If there is not enough quantity available the program should allocate to the customer all of the quantity on hand and back order the remainder. The unit price (before discounts and taxes) is to be used to determine the cost of the item.

2. The customer's record is to be located. It is stored in the Customer Master File. If there is no customer record the transaction is to be treated as an error. A "Create Customer Record" transaction must have been previously received before any customer order transactions can be processed. The customer master record is to be used to determine if

    (a) discount is permitted,
    (b) the amount of the order causes the credit limit permitted to be exceeded, or
    (c) any taxes are to be charged.

3. The amount to be charged for the total order is to be calculated and all taxes and shopping costs are to be included. The order is to be entered on the Customer Order File. The ship-to address and date the order is required are to be checked to see if the shipment can be combined with any previous order. The invoice and bill of lading are to be transferred to the warehouse closest to destination of the goods.

This logic, represented schematically in flow chart form in Figure B.2, is shown in Figures 3a and 3b. The Decision Table is created by using the description of the operational program, and if desired, the high-level flow chart.

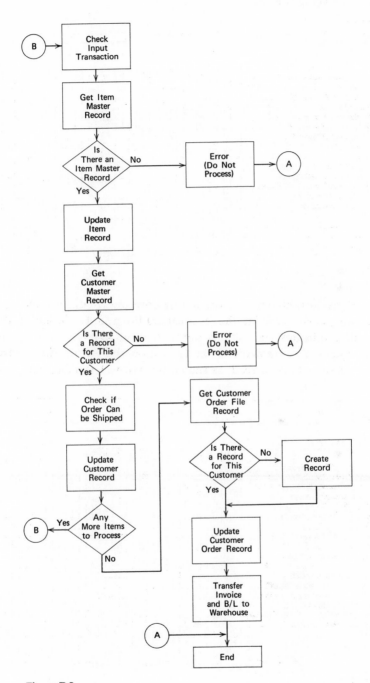

Figure B.2

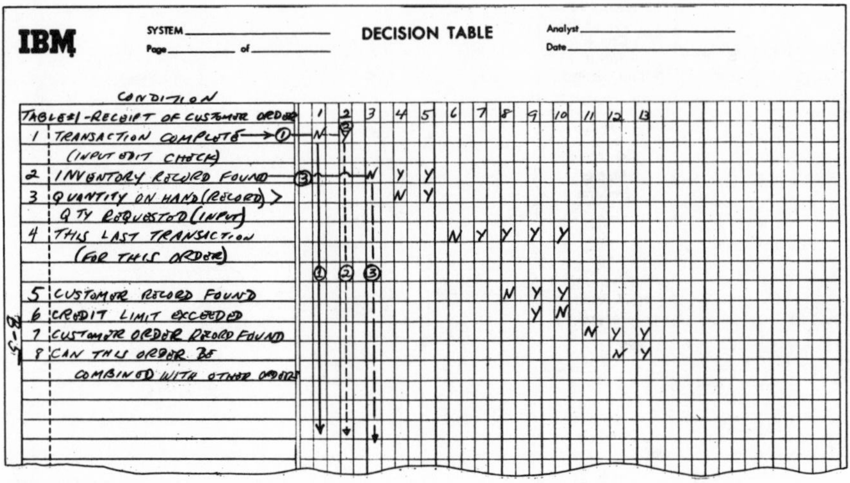

IBM — DECISION TABLE — SYSTEM ____ Page ____ of ____ Analyst ____ Date ____

CONDITION

TABLE #1 - RECEIPT OF CUSTOMER ORDER	1	2	3	4	5	6	7	8	9	10	11	12	13
1 TRANSACTION COMPLETE (INPUT EDIT CHECK) → ①	N	Y											
2 INVENTORY RECORD FOUND ③			N	Y	Y								
3 QUANTITY ON HAND (RECORD) > QTY REQUESTED (INPUT)				N	Y								
4 THIS LAST TRANSACTION (FOR THIS ORDER)						N	Y	Y	Y	Y			
	①	②	③										
5 CUSTOMER RECORD FOUND								N	Y	Y			
6 CREDIT LIMIT EXCEEDED									Y	N			
7 CUSTOMER ORDER RECORD FOUND											N	Y	Y
8 CAN THIS ORDER BE COMBINED WITH OTHER ORDERS												N	Y

Figure B.3a

The decision table was constructed by entering conditions and actions as they were encountered in the Operational Program Logic Specifications. After all conditions and actions were listed, all relevant (not mutually exclusive) entries were made in the Condition and Action Entry Section.

The decision table is read, as shown by Arrow 1 starting with Condi-

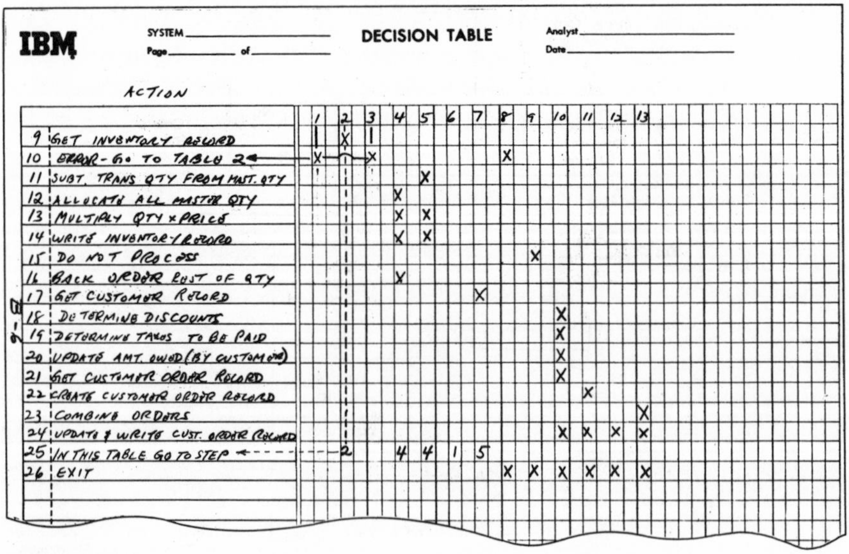

IBM — DECISION TABLE — SYSTEM ____ Page ____ of ____ Analyst ____ Date ____

ACTION

	1	2	3	4	5	6	7	8	9	10	11	12	13
9 GET INVENTORY RECORD		X											
10 ERROR - GO TO TABLE 2	X		X					X					
11 SUBT. TRANS QTY FROM MAST. QTY					X								
12 ALLOCATE ALL MASTER QTY				X									
13 MULTIPLY QTY × PRICE				X	X								
14 WRITE INVENTORY RECORD				X	X								
15 DO NOT PROCESS									X				
16 BACK ORDER REST OF QTY				X									
17 GET CUSTOMER RECORD							X						
18 DETERMINE DISCOUNTS										X			
19 DETERMINE TAXES TO BE PAID										X			
20 UPDATE AMT. OWED (BY CUSTOMER)										X			
21 GET CUSTOMER ORDER RECORD										X			
22 CREATE CUSTOMER ORDER RECORD											X		
23 COMBINE ORDERS													X
24 UPDATE & WRITE CUST. ORDER RECORD										X	X	X	X
25 IN THIS TABLE GO TO STEP		2		4	4	1	5						
26 EXIT								X	X	X	X	X	X

Figure B.3b

tion 1 from left to right until a Yes or No entry is read, down in the Action Entry and left again, to see what actions are to be taken.[2] Arrow 2 flows to Rule 2. Arrow 3 starts with Condition 2 as all relevant conditions for conditions 2 have been reviewed.

The logic of the routine shown in the decision table is not overly complicated. The value of describing the logic on a decision would appear minimal. The logic for Table 2, the error routine shown in Action Stub 10 is more involved. The program logic for this sub-routine is as follows:

1. If the inventory record is not found, request for a retransmission. When the retransmission is received, check the inventory file again only if the second item number is not the same as the one originally received.

2. If they are both the same, send a message back to the sender and to the Sales Department that the item number is invalid. The remainder of the order is to be processed as follows:

   (a) If the customer order record cannot be found but the customer record exists and the credit limit is not exceeded, process the order but note on the output invoice that additional discounts for volume may be applicable.

   (b) If there is a customer order record and no customer record present, process the order but enter it in all items as pending after sending a message to the Sales Department to check the reason why the customer order is missing. If there are more than two items on the order for which there are missing item numbers and there is no customer order record, but there is a customer record, check to see if the items are intended for new models.

In this example, in which the logic is more complicated, it is easier to see the value of a decision table approach to organizing the functions to be performed.

It should be noted that it has been found that there is a resistance to using Decision Tables, when they are first introduced. After an initial adjustment, programmers and analysts begin to appreciate their value.

[2] If desired, the items entered in the action entry of the table can be subscripted, X_1, X_2, etc. (if the sequence of execution of the logic is important).

Index

239

Date Due